JOHN ALLEN'S
TREASURY
OF
MACHINE
KNITTING
STITCHES

A DAVID & CHARLES CRAFT BOOK

To Lilian, my right hand at the Royal College of Art, and
to all the students it has been my privilege to teach

British Library Cataloguing in Publication Data
Allen. John, *1934–*
    John Allen's treasury of machine knitting.
    1. Machine knitting
    I. Title
    746.43'2
    ISBN 0-7153-9364-2

© John Allen 1989

Typeset by ABM Typographics Limited, Hull

Book design by Cooper · Wilson, London

Printed in West Germany by Mohndruck GmbH
for David & Charles Publishers plc
Brunel House   Newton Abbot   Devon

Distributed in the United States by
Sterling Publishing Co. Inc,
2, Park Avenue, New York, NY 10016

CONTENTS

INTRODUCTION

In writing this book I am fulfilling my long held ambition of creating a machine-knitting stitch compendium comparable to the many available for hand knitters. Domestic machine knitting has always been seen as the poor relation of hand knitting, which I resent; it is not, it is simply different; it can be just as creative if the knitter approaches the machine with an open mind and a willingness to experiment. In this book I put forward a few of my personal ideas, a little of my philosophy towards knitting, and hope the reader will thus be led into some of the many interesting and exciting areas of machine knitting. In presenting several ways of knitting one stitch I hope readers will be encouraged to go on developing the structure themselves, eventually arriving at a totally new inspiration of their own.

I believe it does not matter how much technical knowledge you have if you do not know how to use it creatively. A knitter with few technical skills can, if he or she has a creative approach, a flair for colour and an ability to experiment, produce wonderfully attractive fabrics. Obviously the more technical skills one acquires, the more possibilities are opened up, but I want to stress it's not techniques that make creative designers so much as inventiveness, patience and a willingness to try new things. I have a favourite saying 'you do not learn first, then start doing, you learn by doing'. Timidity is the enemy of the knitter; as a wonderful English visionary painter, Cecil Collins, once said, 'neutrality in the face of vision too often wears the mask of mediocrity'. How often does the knitter play safe rather than dare to try a new approach? I always tell my students, 'there is no such word in knitting as don't and no such thing as can't; you must try everything'. It is only by trying out new thoughts and ideas on the machine that the craft of knitting is enhanced and pushed into new exciting regions.

A wide selection of knitting machines is on the market today, each machine having its own unique features making standardised patterns and stitch constructions difficult. Thus you must refer to your own machine manual to get particular instructions on carriage settings which will allow you to knit lace, jacquards etc. I have compiled this book using only a single-bed and 24-stitch repeating structures. This has been done to allow *all* machine knitters to find something to encourage and inspire them. Many of the stitch patterns do not need punchcards and those that do are easily translated onto any of the present punchcard or electronic machines. Whilst all the designs in the book were knitted on a Jones machine, they are equally applicable to all other makes of standard punchcard machines with stitch repeats of 24 needles, ie Knitmaster, Singer, Toyota, etc. All the designs can be used on any electronic machine. Where there is any doubt, refer to the manual for your own machine.

The book is divided into sections, each having a short introduction which highlights the points of importance and interest relating to the particular stitch or structure featured. At the start of most patterns, a tension setting is given; this is only a guide, should you use the type of yarns illustrated in the samples. I break rules, and tension is no exception, so you will find some patterns where fine yarns are used with thick and the tension is set only to accommodate the thick yarn rather than compromise somewhere in between. With reference to cables, I have written these patterns rather than used graphs, simply because many people find this easier to follow and understand.

Many of the most attractive stitch structures are astonishingly simple; do not imagine that all fancy or complicated looking stitches are difficult – they aren't. Most patterns in this book can be knitted by any machine knitter with a little experience who is prepared to have patience and who wants to create something attractive and different. The bane of machine knitters is the need to produce work quickly, lack of confidence in their own abilities and above all, lack of patience. Some of the patterns illustrated are slow to produce, but the resulting fabric is well worth the time spent. Most machine knitters have been brain-washed by machine manufacturers who use quickness of the knitting process on their product as a major selling point. For commercial production this is obviously important, but at least 80 per cent of machine knitters knit for enjoyment not mass production; therefore quality and appearance in the knitting of a garment you otherwise might not be able to afford is much more important than speed.

To gain confidence in experimenting and designing, it is useful to begin with a simple stitch pattern and see how many different interpretations you can knit from it; this is called sampling. Knit two or three inches of your chosen stitch in different colour combinations, using mixtures of smooth and fancy yarns. Tempt yourself into using colours you would not normally use. Play these elements off against each other to create new stitch patterns. Knitting as many different combinations as you can, you should end up with a short scarf-like strip; from this you can select the best and knit these into larger swatches. The importance of sampling cannot be over-emphasised, if you wish to improve your design and colour sense. Only by sampling will you discover your true potential. Do not expect everything to look wonderful; it doesn't, even for the professionals. Always keep your sample strips, they are useful for future reference.

Hand knitters have always been used to combining different stitch patterns, making wonderful confections, but this is not widely practised in machine knitting, mainly because of repeat limitations and the thought of tension changes. But many patterns can be combined very successfully without altering the tension; and sometimes by not changing the tension between different stitch constructions interesting effects, such as seersucker, can be produced. Remember, everything should be tried, there is no such thing as can't in knitting.

For technical reasons it is difficult on most machines to combine stitch constructions horizontally (ie within one row), but vertically many innovations are possible. Try using lace stripes with jacquard, or tuck stitch with patterned stripes. For those knitters with electronic machines more complicated combinations of patterning are possible.

No garment should be started before colour and yarn combinations have been worked out in a variety of ways, to enable a choice of the most attractive to be made. It is important always to save all ends of cones and balls of yarns for this sampling. The best results can never be achieved by going into a yarn supplier's and selecting directly off the shelves the colours you are going to make your garment in, colours need to be seen knitted. Colour is the single most important element of any design; much thought should be given to its selection. To stress the point, go into any department store and watch people coming off the escalator in the dress department. They look around, and, when their eye is caught by an arrangement of colour or colours on a rail, they move over towards it. They then touch the garments, and only if these two initial qualities have satisfied them will they lift the garment off the rail to look at the style and finish.

In any introduction to knitting, some mention should be made of the craft's incredible history. References to knitting go back to the great civilizations of the Egyptians and the Incas in Peru, although more concrete information is available from the Middle Ages onwards. The forming of the great guilds encouraged the craft and its development. In view of the position of knitting today it is interesting to note that these guilds were composed entirely of men, knitting at that time being a male preserve. In England we are lucky in having wonderful examples of hand knitting from these earlier periods right through to contemporary times. Museums such as the City of London, the Victoria and Albert, Leicester Costume, Nottingham Castle and Platt Hall in Manchester, all have marvellous examples. For machine knitting, which entered our craft history much later, there are examples in the museums already mentioned while the Ruddington Framework Knitting Shop Preservation Trust specialises in early machine knitting.

It was men who established the incredibly beautiful knitting on the Aran Isles off Ireland and it was sailors and fishermen who originated much of our traditional knitting. In the nineteenth century the coast of the British Isles seems to have been populated by wonderfully inventive knitters, whole families becoming involved. Out of these village communities came the traditional stitches and styles from which British knitting, in all its rich variety, grew to its world renowned position today. Along the way men lost their dominance, to the extent that it is now thought unmanly to knit and women predominate in the craft. It is only in the last ten years, with the emergence of knitting as a fashion form that male knitters have started to come out of their closets. It no longer really matters what sex the knitter is, only the end result and the constant moving forward of the craft. It is important that knitters today from whatever sex, background or training, all work to build on the fabulous cultural inheritance we are all lucky enough to share, and that there are no 'poor relations', just glorious knitting for all.

TUCK STITCH

Tuck stitch is one of the most three-dimensional constructions which can be produced on the machine; in some patterns it gives an almost sculptural effect. It really consists of a distorting of parts of the knitting by the selected holding of certain stitches while all the rest knit normally. The main effect of this is to create raised surfaces against flat knitted ones. One of the attractions of tuck stitch patterns is that either side of the fabric is equally attractive.

When knitting tuck stitch there is a limit to how many rows you can hold any one stitch over, but only you will know how many that is for you. Some knitters say four rows are the limit, but you will see from the patterns in this section that this is not so. Everything depends on tension, yarn and how you use your yarn carriage. Whether you push it across tentatively or firmly, whether you take it across slowly or quickly, such details are important and can affect the knitting of tuck structures.

The patterns created depend on how the tucking needles have been spaced out – the most commonly used is a brick repeating pattern, which produces a honeycomb effect. This can be elaborated on by the striping in of colour and textured yarns, as illustrated in this section. Tucking does not need to be repeated as a continuous pattern – very pretty effects can be achieved by introducing stocking stitch or small jacquard stripes between areas of tuck stitches.

An interesting experiment to try with tuck stitch is milling or felting. The easiest way to do this is to put the fabric into a washing-machine on an ordinary colour wash (60°F/15°C) using pure soap rather than detergent. When you take the knitting out it will have felted, so that it has a totally different look. Milling can also be done by hand. Use rubber gloves so that you can use really hot water (as little as possible) with pure soap flakes. Rub the fabric vigorously for 7-10 minutes and felting will take place. The results will often be surprising and attractive, but, as in all experiments, there will be some failures until you master the technique. Remember that only wool felts, so if the whole fabric is wool, the whole fabric will felt. Totally different effects can be achieved by using different types of yarns with wool in one swatch. If the tucking stitches are wool and the knitting stitches cotton, the felting will, in effect, make the cotton bubble up rather more than it otherwise would. Try knitting the stitch very loosely and see what effect this produces when the result is felted.

By experimenting with tuck stitch many attractive effects can be produced. Try knitting as many different combinations of one stitch pattern as possible, using different tensions, yarns and colour mixtures. The patterns illustrated in this section will help you to create your own interesting designs.

Important: For punchcard machines, the blanks on the design graphs are punched out. For electronic machines, the design graphs are worked as illustrated and then reversed on the machine. Different makes of machines vary so it is important to consult your own machine manual if you are in doubt.

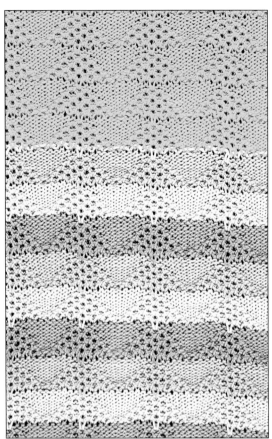

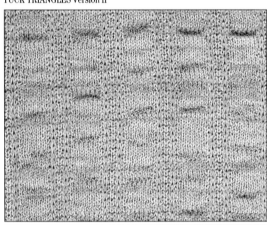

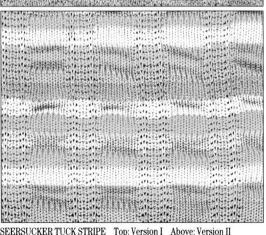

TUCK TRIANGLES Version II

SEERSUCKER TUCK STRIPE   Top: Version I   Above: Version II

TUCK TRIANGLES

Multiples of 24/Tension 7
100% Cotton perle

This design can be knitted as in the graph or it can be halved and single triangles used – ie, a 12-row repeat instead of a 24-row repeat as in the graph.

This stitch can also be changed by doubling up on all the tucking – ie, tuck on 4 stitches instead of just 2 as in the graph. Two different interpretations are illustrated showing the use of colour and striping in the pattern.

Version I

Colour sequence for col A (purple) and col B (pink):
*1 row col A.
  11 rows col B.
  Repeat from *.

Version II

Colour sequence for 3-colour stripe.
*12 rows col A (cream).
  12 rows col B (grey).
  12 rows col C (green).
  Repeat from *.

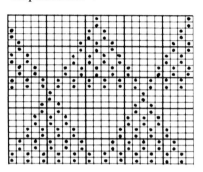

SEERSUCKER TUCK STRIPE

Multiples of 12

Version I

Tension 2
Very fine 3-ply Rabbit hair and cashmere

This tuck stitch creates a wonderful seersucker effect which can be exploited by the use of different yarns, best seen on wrong side of knitting.

Version II

Tension 9
100% Cotton

This is another version of the stitch, but it is shown on the right side. This is done to make the point that many machine-knitted stitches are usable either way.

Colour sequence:
*8 rows col A (pink).
  8 rows col B (lilac).
  8 rows col C (ochre).
  8 rows col D (cream).
  8 rows col E (brown).
  8 rows col F (slate).
  8 rows col G (green).
  8 rows col D.
  Repeat from *.

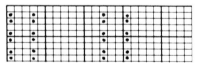

Right: TUCK TRIANGLES Version I

10

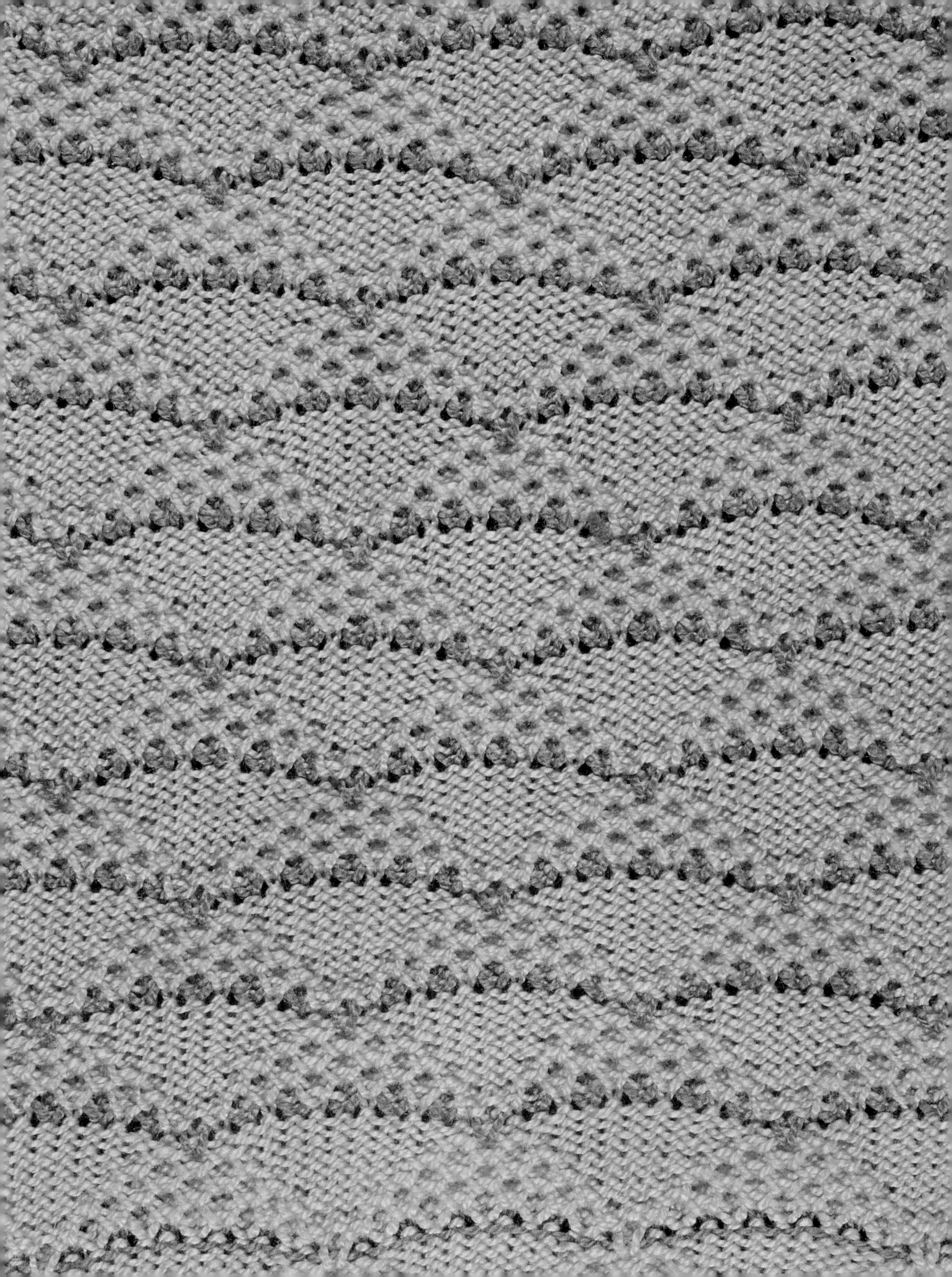

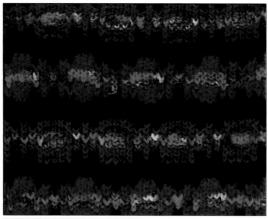

CIRCUITS   Top: Version I   Above: Version II

QUALITY STREET

CIRCUITS

Multiples of 8/Tension 6

Version I
Shetland wool and multi-coloured yarn

  4 rows col A (black).
*4 rows col B (green).
  4 rows col C (multicolour).
  4 rows col B.
  8 rows col A.
  4 rows col D (blue).
  4 rows col C.
  8 rows col A.
  Repeat from *.

This pattern is ideal for experimenting with colour and textured yarns.

The second version of the pattern demonstrates how different it looks simply by changing the colours and colour sequence.

Version II
4-ply Acrylic

Colour sequence:
  2 rows col A (green).
  2 rows col B (navy).
  2 rows col C (yellow).
  2 rows col B.
  2 rows col A.
  2 rows col D.

This sequence forms the colour repeat. The complete pattern and colour repeat is over 72 rows.

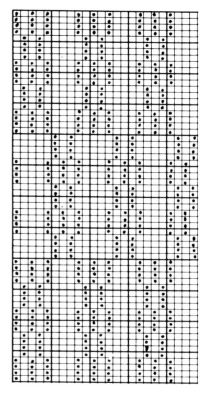

QUALITY STREET

Multiples of 12/Tension 5-6
100% 4-ply Acrylic

Colour sequence as illustrated:
4 rows col A (dark blue).
4 rows col B (pink).
4 rows col A.
4 rows col C (red).

This forms the repeat, except that col C is changed each time over 4 repeats of the pattern before starting at the beginning again.

The appearance of this design can be completely changed by using just 2 colours, knitted as follows:
*4 rows col A.
 12 rows col B.
 Repeat from *.

This looks particularly attractive if a textured yarn is used as col A.

Try your own combinations and create an individual look for this stitch. I have called it Quality Street because it was inspired by sweet-wrappers.

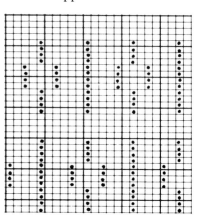

MOTH

Multiples of 6/Tension 4-5

Version I

100% Cotton perle

The swatch illustrated uses cotton perle yarn. To make this stitch more interesting, knit the following colourways, not illustrated here:

Version II

*Row 1: textured yarn.
 Rows 2 and 3: straight yarn.
 Row 4: textured yarn.
 Repeat from*.

Version III

*Row 1: black looped yarn.
 Rows 2, 3 and 4: white yarn.
 Repeat from *.

From these 2 colour sequences try your own combinations. Remember that the colour repeat need not repeat over just 4 rows, but you could make the colour repeat over multiples of 4 – ie, 8, 12 or 16.

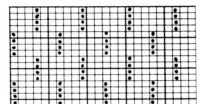

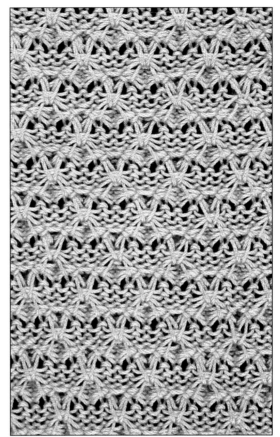

MOTH Version I

BLOCKED SQUARES

Multiples of 6/Tension 6

Version I

100% Cotton perle

The swatch illustrated uses cotton perle yarn. At the bottom of the swatch is an example of what happens if you reduce the number of rows in a block. Experiment with different combinations of rows to produce multisized blocks in one design.

This pattern can be enhanced and be made to appear very complicated by the imaginative use of colour and yarn in the following ways, not illustrated here:

Version II

Use a 2nd colour and textured yarn and insert it on the 1st, 14th, 15th and 28th row of the repeat.

Version III

Use as many bright or soft colours as you have and colour the pattern in blocks of 14 rows. This will give you a multicoloured checkerboard effect.

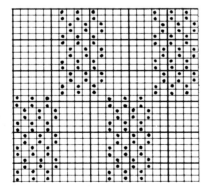

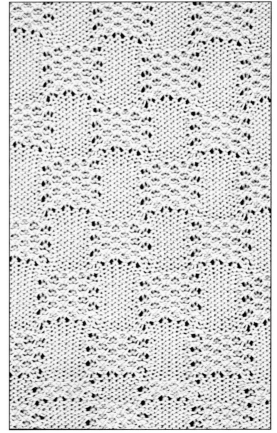

BLOCKED SQUARES Version I

SCOTTISH LANDSCAPE

Multiples of 8/Tension 6
100% Acrylic and 100% wool

This stitch gives a subtle raised effect which can be exaggerated by using cotton or wools.

Colour sequence:
*1 row col A (white wool).
 2 rows col B (multi-coloured acrylic).
 Repeat from *.

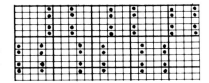

MICRODOT

Multiples of 6/Tension 4-5
3- or 4-ply Acrylic/mohair mix

This is a small simple design but it can be made to look extremely interesting by the use of colour. Try changing the colour every 2 rows, or use 1 colour as standard but change the 2nd colour on every alternate 2 rows. You will soon see how you can develop this pattern to make it special.

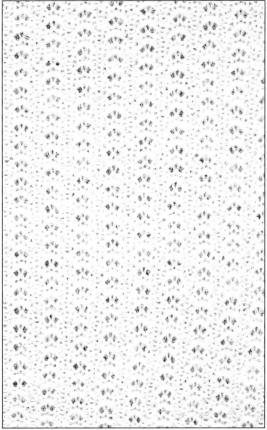
MICRODOT

SPOT STITCH

Multiples of 24/Tension 8
Shetland wool with wool and mohair

This design can be worked in any yarn.

With this particular combination, a good raised effect is achieved. This design knitted in a matt and shiny yarn could look good – eg, cotton and rayon.

Remember to keep the rayon as the main colour as it is always difficult to tuck with, especially over as many rows as this.

Colour sequence:
*2 rows col A (white wool).
 8 rows col B (navy).
 2 rows col A.
 8 rows col C (purple).
 2 rows col A.
 8 rows col D (dark heather).
 2 rows col A.
 8 rows col E (lilac).
 2 rows col A.
 8 rows col F (blue).
 Repeat from *.

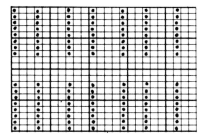

SPOT STITCH

Left: SCOTTISH LANDSCAPE

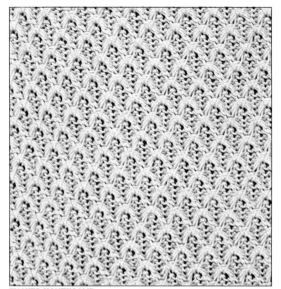

TUCKED HONEYCOMB

SKYSCRAPER

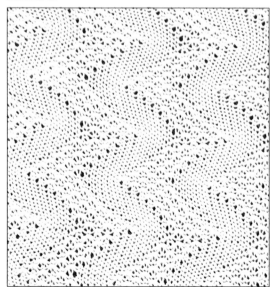

ZIG-ZAG TUCK

TUCKED HONEYCOMB

Multiples of 3/Tension 6
100% Cotton perle

The right side of this pattern is rather uninteresting, but the wrong side is an elaborate honeycomb-type structure which looks rich and thick.

The fabric produced, however, is light and airy – ideal for summer sweaters. To make a winter version, use wool or kid mohair to achieve the same richness.

The repeat is worked over 3 stitches and 18 rows. However, the repeat is broken down, as you can see from the graph, into sets of 6 rows. Use this if you want to introduce 2 or 3 colours. By changing colour at the end of every 6th row, an interesting kaleidoscope effect can be produced.

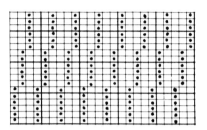

SKYSCRAPER

Multiples of 12/Tension 5
4-ply Acrylic

This design uses the tuck stitch and complements it with areas of plain flat knitting which gives a rich textured surface to the fabric. Colour has been introduced to exaggerate the three-dimensional effect. This could be further developed by experimenting with more colour and different colour changes.

Colour sequence:
*4 rows col A (navy).
 2 rows col B (green).
 Repeat from *.

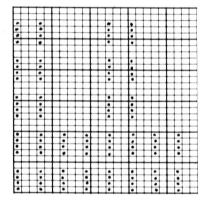

ZIG-ZAG TUCK

Multiples of 12/Tension 4-5
100% Cotton perle

A single one-colour tucked zig-zag is shown. It could be made more colourful and interesting if you did not want the softness of the design by using different yarns of 1 colour and changing them every 2 rows.

A further alternative would be to knit a textured yarn on the 2 rows of pattern where the zig-zag changes direction – ie, rows 12 and 13.

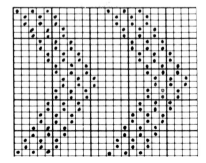

TUCKED HOLES

Multiples of 2/Tension 4-5
100% Cotton perle

By altering the tension, the appearance of this pattern can be changed radically, as it can by the use of colour. While these designs are knitted in 100% cotton, the pattern works well in other yarns. If you are willing to experiment with single row knitting, try a sequence as follows:

*1 row col A.
3 rows col B.
1 row col A.
3 rows col C.
Repeat from *.

Colour sequence illustrated:
*4 rows col A (yellow).
4 rows col B (green).
4 rows col C (red).
4 rows col D (turquoise).
4 rows col E (purple).
4 rows col F (pink).
Repeat from *.

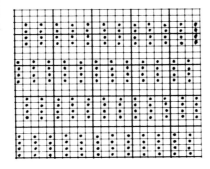

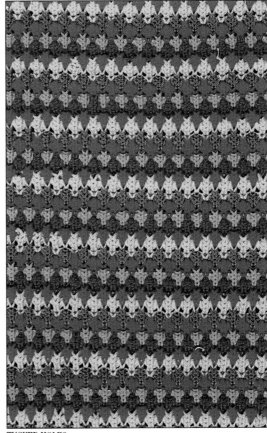

TUCKED HOLES

ELONGATED DIAMONDS

Multiples of 24/Tension 5-6
100% 4-ply Wool

The tension is critical in knitting this design. If you have too tight a tension for the yarn you choose to knit in, seersucker effects are developed in the centre of the diamonds. This can look very interesting and can also be exaggerated by tightening the tension as much as practical. The looser the tension the less raised the tuck stitches will be and so the design will appear flatter but still interesting.

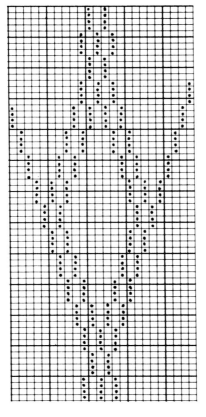

ELONGATED DIAMONDS

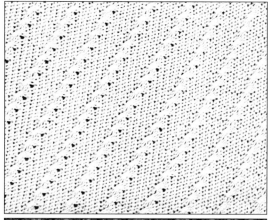

TUCKED STRIPE Top: Version I Above: Version II

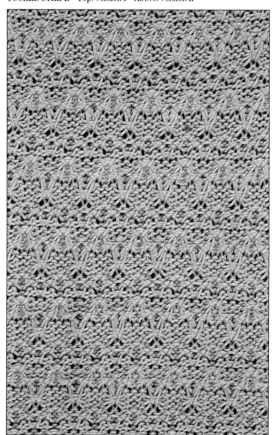

TUCKED LACE

TUCKED STRIPE

Multiples of 6/Tension 3

Version I

100% Rayon

This simple diagonal stripe looks very effective when knitted in rayon as the yarn catches and reflects the light where the tucking takes place.

Version II

Tension 5
100% Cotton

This sample illustrates how totally different the same design can look if colour is introduced. This pattern is knitted with 3 rows col A (blue), 1 row col B (green).

It is worth using the odd row colour change, because by using only 1 row of col B, a 2nd diagonal stripe appears, running in the opposite direction to the tucking stripe.

Try other combinations and produce your own interpretation of this by the creative use of colour.

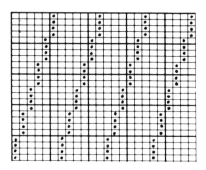

TUCKED LACE

Multiples of 4/Tension 6
100% Cotton perle

A very simple but effective tuck stitch, ideal for experimentation. This stitch, because of its structure, would produce very rich complicated colour effects. Play around with feeding different colours and yarns into the pattern and see how you can develop the fabric.

Suggestion 1: introduce a 2nd colour on rows 1, 5 and 9.

Suggestion 2: introduce a 2nd colour and textured yarn on rows 1 and 2, 5 and 6, 9 and 10, 13 and 14.

Suggestion 3: using 6 colours, feed them in as follows:
*4 rows col A.
 4 rows col B.
 4 rows col C.
 2 rows col D.
 2 rows col E.
 2 rows col F.
 Repeat from *.

You can work many colour combinations using suggestion 3 as your starting point.

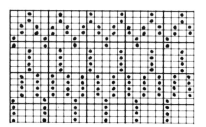

DIAGONAL PLOUGH

Multiples of 12/Tension 7
100% Cotton perle

This tuck stitch is extremely simple and based on 2 and 4 tucked stitches. Colour experimentation can be most interesting if the colour or textured yarns are used in multiples of 2 or 4. For the adventurous knitter with patience, try feeding the colour in as follows: 3 rows col A, 1 row col B. This way of colouring will give you a totally different effect from using the colours in even numbers.

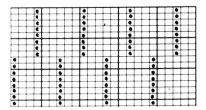

DIAGONAL PLOUGH

QUILT TUCK

Multiples of 6/Tension 8
100% Wool

This is a large tuck which gives a dramatic three-dimensional effect. Both sides of the fabric are interesting enough to be used. Try using a textured yarn instead of the white in the illustration or a shiny rayon yarn. Either can enhance the appearance of the pattern.

QUILT TUCK

COLLAGE

Multiples of 24/Tension 5-6
100% Acrylic

This pattern has a subtle raised effect, which if knitted in 100% wool can be exaggerated by altering the tension and yarn combinations.

Colour sequence:
*2 rows col A (red).
 4 rows col B (navy).
 2 rows col A.
 2 rows col B.
 2 rows col C (green).
 Repeat from *.

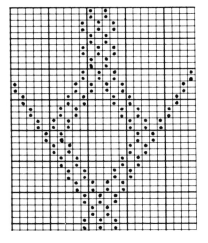

COLLAGE

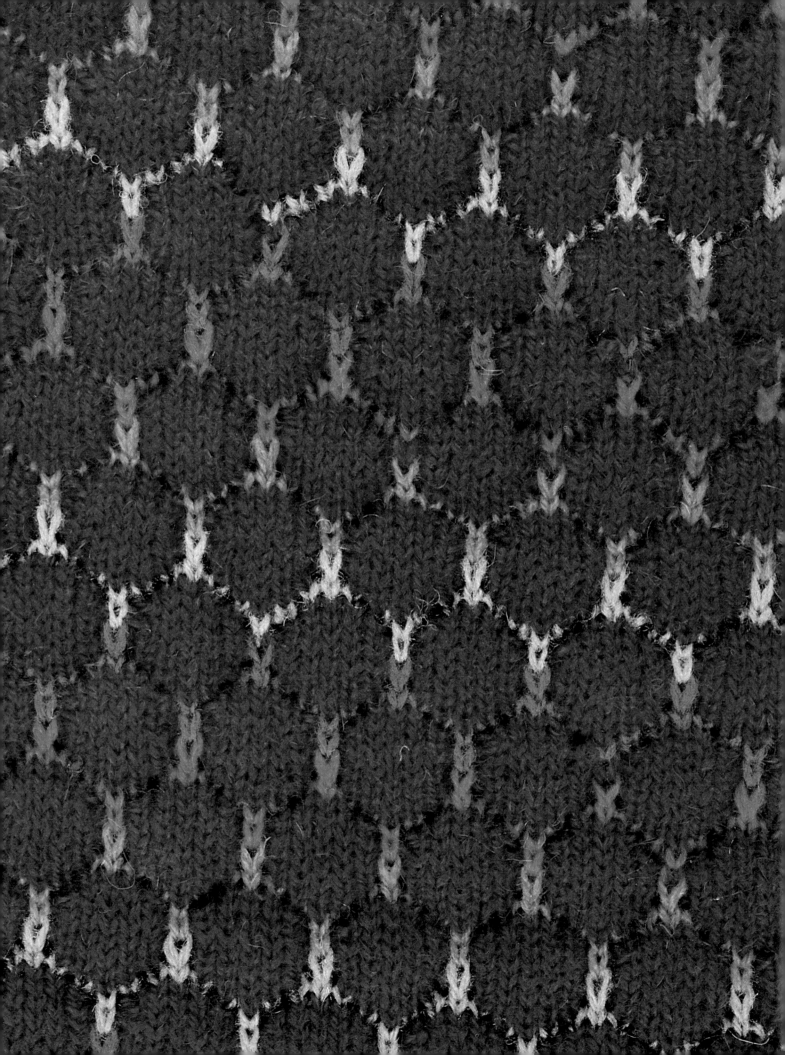

CIRCLE TUCK

Multiples of 6/Tension 8

Each side of the fabric is attractive in this three-dimensional design. It provides great scope for experimentation, particularly with the way colour is fed into the pattern. By altering or using less colours, very different patterns can be achieved.

Version I

Shetland wool

Colour sequence:
*8 rows col A (blue).
 2 rows col B (green).
 8 rows col A.
 2 rows col C (red).
 8 rows col A.
 2 rows col D (lilac).
 8 rows col A.
 2 rows col E (yellow).
 Repeat from *.

Version II

White wool and lurex

*8 rows col A (white).
 2 rows col B (lurex).
 Repeat from *.

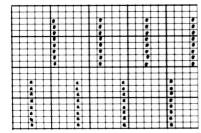

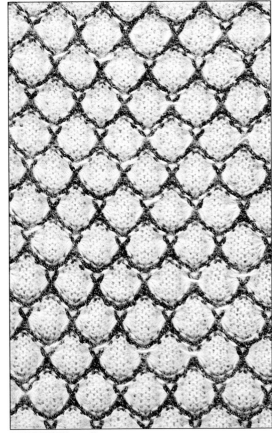

CIRCLE TUCK Version II

STONE WALL

Multiples of 12/Tension 5
100% Acrylic

This pattern is made by tucking over 12 rows.

Because of this huge tuck the pattern should only be knitted in really soft wools – ie, botany wool, lambswool, or soft acrylic as illustrated.

Colour sequence:
*4 rows col A (green).
 4 rows col B (yellow).
 4 rows col A.
 4 rows col C (orange).
 12 rows col B.
 4 rows col C.
 Repeat from *.

Try changing the colours. You could also change the yarns to any you like with the exception of that used in place of col C. This must always be a soft yarn for the reasons already explained.

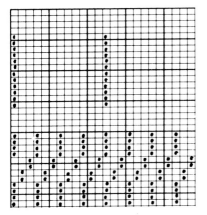

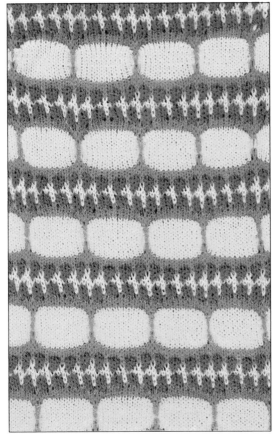

STONE WALL

Left: CIRCLE TUCK Version I

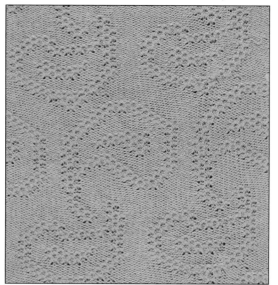

PAISLEY

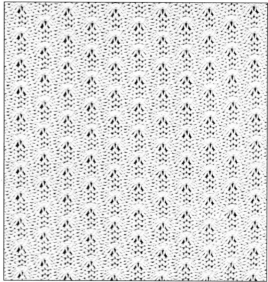

BARLEY TUCK

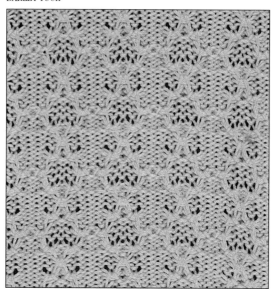

BUTTERFLY TUCK

PAISLEY

Multiples of 24/Tension 4
100% Cotton perle

This design works very well in any yarn. By tightening the tension the raised effect is emphasised. Obviously this also affects the handle of the fabric, so you have to discover what tension is best for both with the yarn you choose to work in.

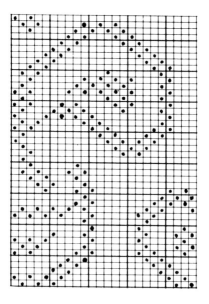

BARLEY TUCK

Multiples of 6/Tension 5
100% Cotton perle

This simple tuck stitch gives a wonderful effect on the right side of the fabric and a little butterfly effect texture on the wrong side of the fabric. Either is attractive. With creative making up, both sides could be used in one garment to great effect. Experiment with colour over the stitch repeat of 4 rows, which could yield interesting results.

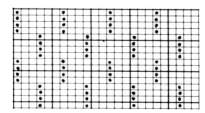

BUTTERFLY TUCK

Multiples of 6/Tension 6
100% Cotton perle

The tension on this pattern is important. It is rather looser than normal and exaggerates the floats created by the tucking. The looser floats create the butterfly wing shapes which are so pretty.

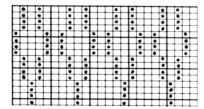

CRAZY PAVING

Multiples of 24/Tension 5
100% Acrylic

This design works just as well in 100% wool, but could be tried in mixtures of yarns.

The important thing to remember is that the yarn used in place of col A should have a certain amount of elasticity in it, as this is used on the tucking needles.

Colour sequence:
*2 rows col A (navy).
 2 rows col B (orange).
 6 rows col C (green).
 2 rows col A.

2 rows col C.
6 rows col B.
Repeat from *.

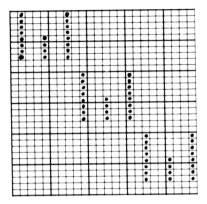

TUCKED LADDERS

Version I
Multiples of 3/Tension 7
100% Wool

Colour sequence:
*4 rows col A (white).
 2 rows col B (black).
 Repeat from *.

This design in wool gives a neat appearance with the white tucks well raised (not illustrated).

The appearance can be altered by reducing the number of stitches between the tucking stitch or by increasing the number of plain rows between them.

Version II
Multiples of 4/Tension 5
100% Cotton perle

This extension of the tucked ladder illustrates one of the subtle changes which take place simply by adding 1 extra stitch into the

repeat (repeat over 4 needles instead of 3) and knitting the pattern in a range of colours.

Colour sequence:
*4 rows col A (lilac).
 2 rows col B (rust).
 4 rows col C (sage).
 2 rows col B.
 4 rows col D (lime).
 2 rows col B.
 4 rows col E (grey).
 2 rows col B.
 4 rows col F (peach).
 2 rows col B.
 4 rows col G (green).
 2 rows col B.
 4 rows col H (pink).
 2 rows col B.
 Repeat from *.

You can use as few or as many colours as you wish, but col B is the same throughout. Try different combinations until you find one you really like.

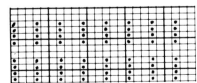

Version I

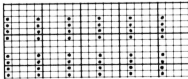

Version II

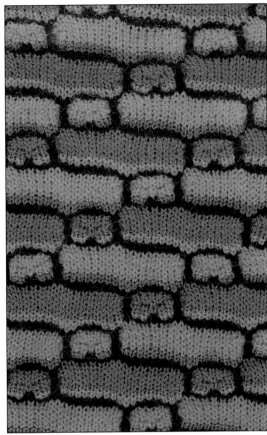

CRAZY PAVING

TUCKED LADDERS Version II

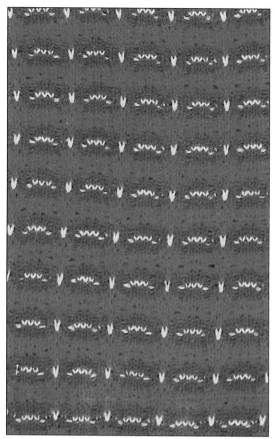

NOSTALGIA

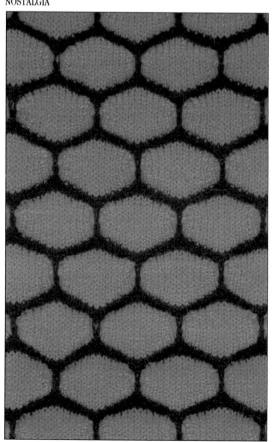

BEEHIVE

NOSTALGIA

Multiples of 8/Tension 6
Shetland wool

This is an extremely versatile pattern for experimentation with yarns and colour. Illustrated here is an unusual colouring to show how effective 1 row of a contrasting colour can be (ie, yellow.) The problem with odd rows is the ends which need dealing with on the finished fabric, but sometimes as here the design is worth the work.

Also note that needles have been pushed out of work to give a ladder effect. These needles are pushed out of work only after the pattern needles have been selected on the 1st row to allow you to position the design correctly.

Colour sequence:
*3 rows col A (purple).
 1 row col B (yellow).
 3 rows col A.
 17 rows col C (red).
 Repeat from *.

On the graph, NWP is indicated by ⟨.

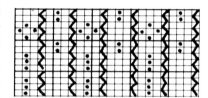

BEEHIVE

Multiples of 12/Tension 5
100% Acrylic

This is a huge tuck stitch – the tuck, in fact, is held over 12 rows. Because of this, soft acrylic yarn must be used. This stitch does not work with wool or cotton.

The cloth produced looks very thick, but it has a good handle and is extremely light in weight – obviously an ideal stitch with which to experiment. Use a fancy yarn or multicoloured yarn for the sets of 4 rows not tucking and see the rich effect produced.

Colour sequence:
*4 rows col A (navy).
 12 rows col B (pink).
 Repeat from *.

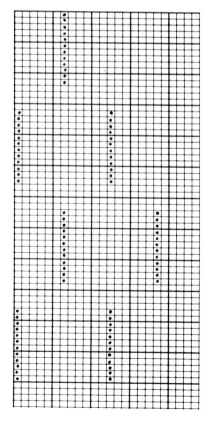

FAIRGROUND

Multiples of 12/Tension 4-5
4-ply Acrylic multicolour and cotton perle

This pattern can be knitted in any yarn, but cotton with acrylic as used here works best because of their different qualities. Cotton – having little elasticity – gives a very three-dimensional effect when tucked with acrylic which behaves in the opposite way. The tension used is dictated by the cotton which should be knitted as tightly as possible to achieve the best three-dimensional effects.

Colour sequence:
*8 rows col A (multicolour acrylic).
 6 rows col B (navy cotton).
 Repeat from *.

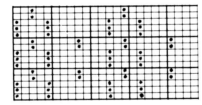

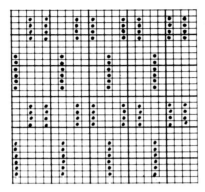
FAIRGROUND

DAISY TUCK STRIPE

Multiples of 24/Tension 5
100% Cotton perle

This design looks very exciting if striped in different colours.
The same stitch could be knitted by doubling up the tucking stitches and altering the tension accordingly.

Colour sequence:
*2 rows col A.
 3 rows col B.
 Repeat from *.

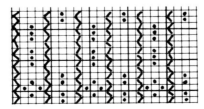

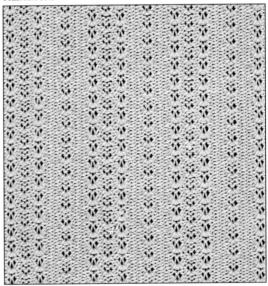
DAISY TUCK STRIPE

SNAKES AND LADDERS

Multiples of 8/Tension 5
100% Cotton perle

The open lace of this tuck stitch is created by taking the needles out of work.
On the 1st row of needle selection, transfer the stitch on either side of the 2 tucking stitches to the adjacent needle and push empty needle to NWP. The needle set-out should then appear as ·111·111·111·. It is important not to set the needles before you have seen the pattern selection, other-wise it is easy to get the NWP needles in the wrong place on the pattern.

On the graph, NWP is indicated by ⟨.

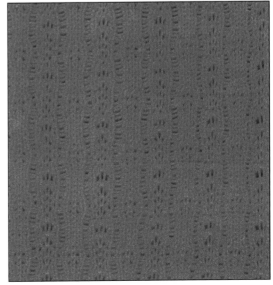
SNAKES AND LADDERS

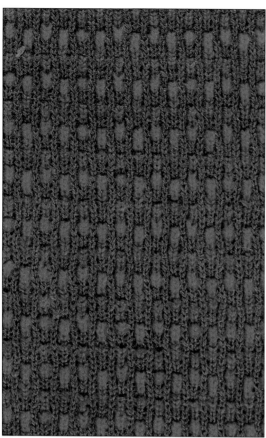

TUCKED TWEED Version II

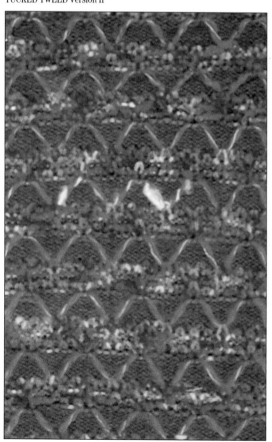

CARNIVAL

TUCKED TWEED

Multiples of 4/Tension 7
Shetland wool

This little tweed tuck stitch is very versatile.

Here are 2 of the many designs that can be produced from this stitch simply by experimenting with the colour sequence. Try textured yarns as they will give an added richness.

Version I
*4 rows col A (green).
 4 rows col B (purple).
 4 rows col A.
 4 rows col C (red).
 Repeat from *.

Version II
*4 rows col A (purple).
 4 rows col B (green).
 4 rows col C (red).
 4 rows col B.
 Repeat from *.

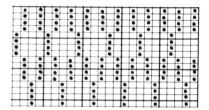

CARNIVAL

Multiples of 8/Tension 6
Shetland wool, multicolour acrylic and chunky mohair

K 10 rows col A (multicolour).
Set for tuck and start pattern.
*Change to col B (green) and K 2 rows, then with col C (chunky mohair laying in yarn) hook the yarn around each needle selected (every 8th needle).
K 6 rows.
Change to col A, then pick up loops of col C and hook them over needles directly above (every 8th needle) across the knitting.
K 10 rows and repeat from *.

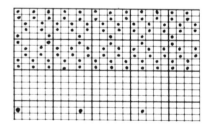

Right: TUCKED TWEED Version I

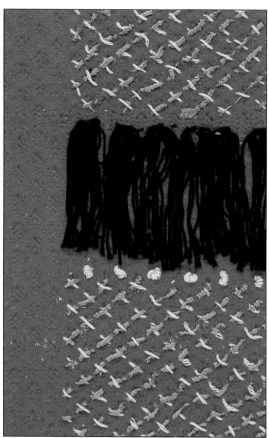

CRISS-CROSS TUCK

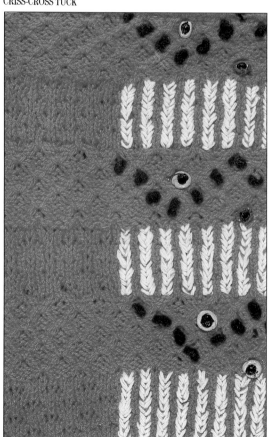

TRANSFERRED TUCK

CRISS-CROSS TUCK

Multiples of 4/Tension 7
100% Cotton

Set for tuck and K as graph.

*K 53 rows, then lock PC for 1 row.
Release PC and K 49 rows.
Lock PC and set for normal knitting.
K 4 rows. Pick up every 5th st from 1st row of plain knitting and put it back on the needles.
Set for tuck and repeat from *.

To attach the fringe to the knitting, use the loops of the sts formed by picking up the 5th st. The criss-cross pattern is made by threading yellow and green cotton through the tuck stitches in diagonal lines, each colour in a different direction (see illustration for guidance). To finish, French knots are sewn into the tuck sts where the 1 row of plain was knitted. The sample shows the knitting before and after decoration.

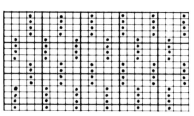

TRANSFERRED TUCK

Multiples of 4/Tension 7
100% Cotton

*Set for tuck and K 21 rows of the PC. Turn knitting around by using garter bar or by hand so the reverse of the fabric is facing you. Repeat from *.

To decorate as illustrated, Swiss darn (see p174) in yellow cotton over alternate columns of sts on the face side of the tuck st. On the reverse side of the tuck, sew French knots in a zig-zag line using the tuck pattern as guidance and add beads in between.

Very simple stitch patterns can be turned into very interesting designs by decorating in this way. You could easily design your own patterns which do not involve turning the fabric around every 21 rows.

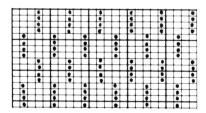

RIPPLE TUCK

Multiples of 4/Tension 7
100% Cotton perle

This is a simple pattern but very effective and easy to vary. While the pattern is worked over 7 rows here, which means breaking yarn and many ends to deal with when the knitting is finished, a similar design can be achieved by changing the colour sequence to 8 or 6 row repeats.

Colour sequence:
*7 rows col A (blue).

7 rows col B (plum).
7 rows col C (purple).
7 rows col D (rust).
Repeat from *.

Reverse of fabric shown.

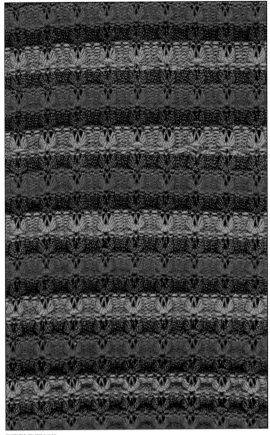

RIPPLE TUCK

DIAMOND TUCK

Multiples of 24/Tension 5-6
Cotton perle

This design can be developed by changing the colours on rows 15 and 24 or by adding textured yarns. These could be knitted in every 2 rows, ie, 2 rows straight yarn, 2 rows textured yarn. Try your own combinations.

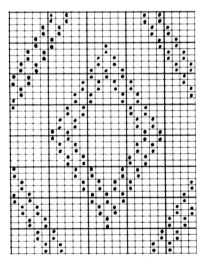

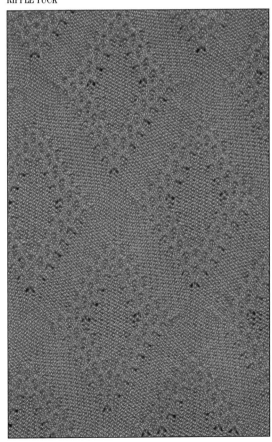

DIAMOND TUCK

29

LACE

Lace can be produced by hand transfer using hand-transfer tools, or by automatic stitch transfer, the latter being carried out by means of a special lace carriage or a facility which you switch into for knitting it on the normal carriage. This will be explained in the manual supplied by the machine manufacturer.

Knitted lace is produced by creating a series of holes which are formed by transferring stitches from one needle to another, leaving the empty needles in the working position. On the next row all the stitches are knitted, new stitches being formed on the empty needles. A variety of patterns can be made according to which needles are used for transferring the stitches.

Although lace knitting has been produced in Europe from the fifteenth century, it was not until the eighteenth century, with the importing of fine cotton from the East, that it became popular – at the time it was called 'white knitting' because of the colour and fine quality of the spun yarn. Many examples of white knitting survive from this period. In the nineteenth century, very finely spun wool was produced in the Shetland Islands, which led to the knitting of the now famous Shetland lace and shawls. Most examples of historical lace knitting were worked by hand, but these examples provide the designer/machine knitter with a wonderful source of new design ideas. Practically any lace stitch can be altered and modified to change its appearance. The simplest step in developing your own design from a pattern is to break the lace up by adding stripes of stocking stitch between stripes of lace. This can be done horizontally or vertically. This easy introduction to developing a design idea is ideal for boosting your confidence and for assisting you to originate your own new patterns.

As all the designs in this section were knitted on a Jones/Brother machine, readers using other machines will need to adapt the patterns by consulting their machine manuals. Knitmaster owners can use the graphs as they are illustrated, but the designs produced will appear slightly different from the swatches shown.

Important: For punchcard machines, the blanks on the design graphs are punched out. For electronic machines, the design graphs are worked as illustrated and then reversed on the machine. Different makes of machines vary so it is important to consult your own machine manual if you are in doubt.

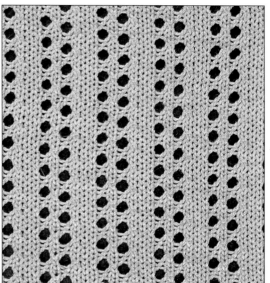

BLOCKED LACE

BLOCKED LACE

Multiples of 24/Tension 6
100% Acrylic

This design is versatile if the knitter wishes to be inventive with it. The pattern can easily be broken into different sections.

The Lace Interlock design on page 35 is, in fact, part of this design simply put into a half-drop repeat.

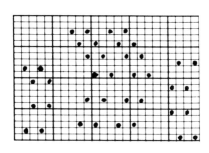

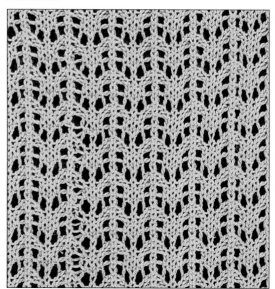

LACE STRIPE

LACE STRIPE

Multiples of 6/Tension 5
100% Cotton

This is an extremely versatile stitch and many more designs can be created from it. Simply by adding and subtracting knitted rows between the lace stitch transfer rows, different stripe, block and check patterns can be invented.

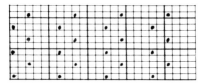

HORSESHOE

Multiples of 6/Tension 7
100% Cotton

In this lace design the stitches are transferred to both right and left, which distorts the stitch forms and holes into pretty horseshoe shapes. You can develop this pattern by striping colour into it every 14 rows – ie, 1 complete repeat.

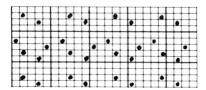

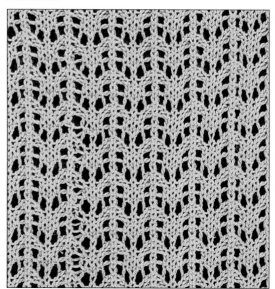

HORSESHOE

SINGLE AND DOUBLE STRIPES

Multiples of 6/Tension 8

Version 1
100% Cotton gimp

Not illustrated, this version is knitted as the graph. The choice of yarns is important as heavy twist yarns will distort the stripe diagonally. This is an ideal pattern to experiment with and develop your own ideas.

Version II
100% Rayon and chenille

In the development shown here, plain knitted rows have been added between the lace rows. Knit as in graph.

Colour sequence:
*6 rows col A (rust rayon).
 2 rows col B (beige chenille).
 Repeat from *.

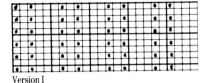

Version I

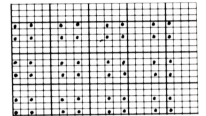

Version II

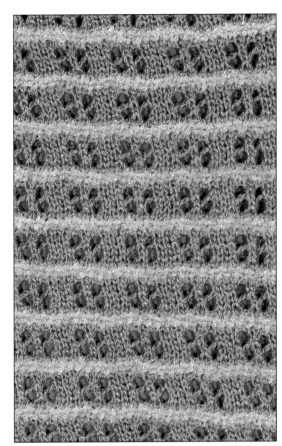

SINGLE AND DOUBLE STRIPES Version II

ROUNDEL

Multiples of 12 needles/Tension 6
100% Shetland wool

Added colour can totally transform this design. Try using 2 or 4 colours and changing these on every 3rd, 10th, 14th and 21st rows. Once you have understood the pattern and colour changes, try your own, perhaps only using a colour for 2 rows at a time. A suggestion for further colour experimentation is set out below.

Colour sequence changed on 1st row after lace rows:

*Row 1: col A.
 Rows 2, 3 and 4: col B.
 Rows 5, 6, 7 and 8: col C.
 Rows 9, 10 and 11: col A.
 Row 12: col B.
 Rows 13, 14 and 15: col A.
 Rows 16, 17, 18 and 19: col C.
 Rows 20, 21 and 22: col B.
 Repeat from *.

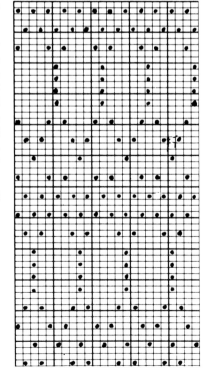

ROUNDEL

ZEBRA STRIPE

ZEBRA STRIPE

Multiples of 6/Tension 5-6
100% Cotton perle

For an experiment, try knitting Zebra Stripe in 2 rows of black then 2 rows of white alternately. A further interesting development of this pattern is to knit it in a gimp yarn (tweed is best). A completely different effect is achieved which gives the already heavily textured surface even more richness. This is a good design on which to use fabric crayons or paints to decorate the stocking-stitch areas.

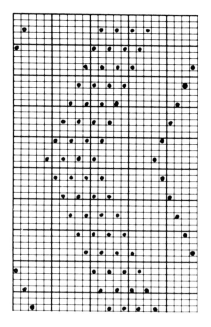

LACE LEAVES

Multiples of 12/Tension 4-5
100% Cotton

This is a very attractive stitch knitted in one colour as illustrated. A really beautiful effect can be achieved if small flowers are painted in fabric paint or crayon on the flat diamond-shaped areas sandwiched between the lace leaf shapes.

By threading ribbon through the lace holes around the leaf shapes, you can produce an even richer looking fabric.

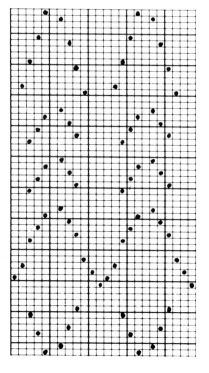

LACE LEAVES

LACE INTERLOCK

Multiples of 12/Tension 8
100% Wool

With this very pretty design, experimenting with colour and textured yarns will pay dividends.

Just one interpretation is illustrated. Try some of your own before deciding on which way to knit this pattern.

*6 rows col A (white).
 2 rows col B (multicolour).
 Repeat from *.

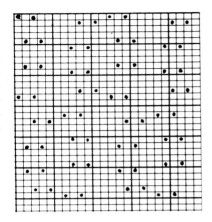

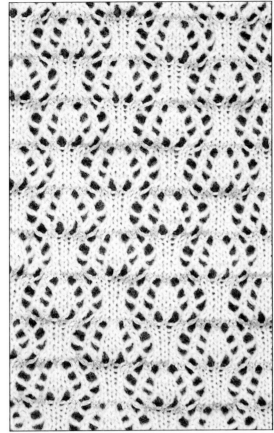

LACE INTERLOCK

LACE SQUARES

Multiples of 8/Tension 6
100% Cotton gimp

It is obvious from looking at this design that colour could be added to great effect between the lace squares; the more colour, the richer the effect produced.

Version I
Cotton gimp
Set carriage for lace. K as graph.

Version II
At the 1st needle selection, transfer onto next needle the centre st of every set of 3 separating the lace blocks. Push the empty needle into the NWP.

Colour sequence:
*12 rows col A (yellow cotton).
 2 rows col B (pink rayon tape yarn).
 Repeat from *.

When the swatch is complete, thread col B through the alternate loops of the ladder made by the needle out of work.

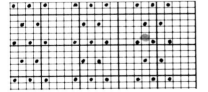

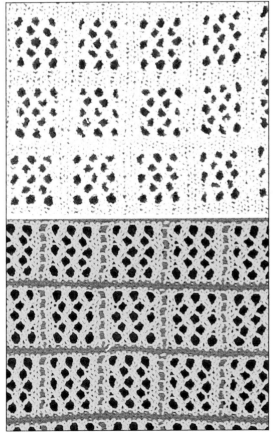

LACE SQUARES: Top: Version I   Above: Version II

LACE CHEVRON

Multiples of 12/Tension 6

This is a very easy and simple pattern which you can experiment with in a variety of ways.

Versions II and III are illustrated.

Version I

Shetland wool

Work as graph in solid colour.

Version II

100% Cotton

Work as graph but with 2 extra rows of plain knitting between repeats. This is to allow for the colour striping repeat. (These 2 extra rows are shown at the top of the graph.)

Colour sequence:
*6 rows col A (cream).
4 rows col B (grey/green).
6 rows col A.
2 rows col C (light green).
6 rows col A.
4 rows col B.
6 rows col A.
2 rows col D (mustard).
Repeat from *.

Version III

100% Cotton with rayon tape

Work as graph but with 4 rows of plain added to the top of the repeat, giving 6 rows of plain between repeats of lace. This version is knitted in 1 colour and, when complete, 2 ends of rayon tape are threaded through alternate holes of the lace to give a rich embroidered look. Any thick-textured yarn or ribbon can be used for the threading. Again, experiment until you get a good effect.

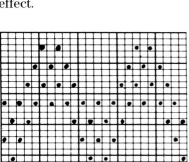

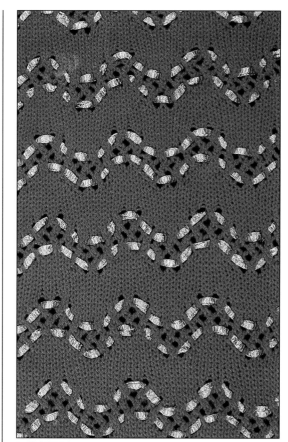

LACE CHEVRON Version III

LACE PAVING

Multiples of 24/Tension 5.5
4-ply Rayon knitted yarn

This design, although knitted here in multicoloured yarn, looks good in cotton and wools. You can also introduce colour by striping it in on the last and first stitches of the small circular shape – ie, rows 1 to 8 of the lace.

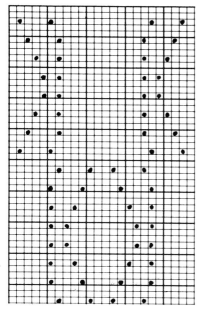

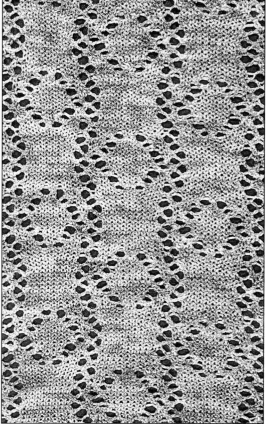

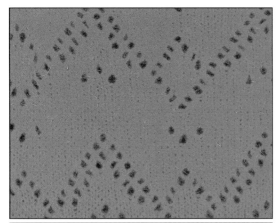

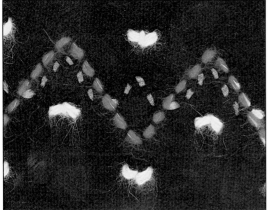

ZIG-ZAG   Top: Version I   Above: Version II

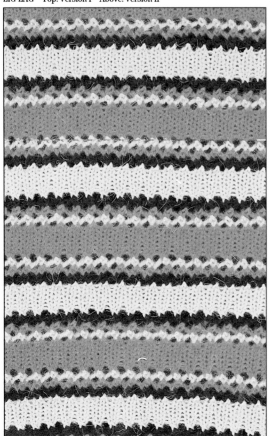

STRIPY LACE

ZIG-ZAG

Multiples of 24

Version I
Tension 6
100% Wool and acrylic

Here the design is worked in a single colour as an all-over pattern.

Version II
Tension 6
4-ply wool, mohair, angora and rayon tape yarn.

This is worked by knitting the pattern just once and, when the desired length has been completed, threading coloured yarns through the holes made by the lace. Fancy textured yarns can also be used. The illustration shows yellow angora used with green rayon tape yarn and pink mohair, all on black 4-ply wool. This is suitable as a border.

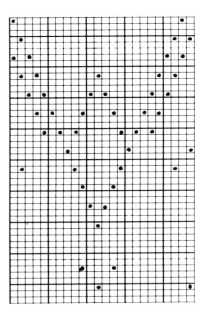

STRIPY LACE

Multiples of 6/Tension 5
100% 4-ply Acrylic

This is another lace pattern where colours and textured yarns can be used to create an elaborate-looking surface fabric which in reality consists of an extremely simple stitch.

Colour sequence:
*2 rows col A (navy).
 2 rows col B (orange).
 2 rows col C (yellow).
 8 rows col B.
 2 rows col C.
 2 rows col B.
 2 rows col A.
 8 rows col C.
 Repeat from *.

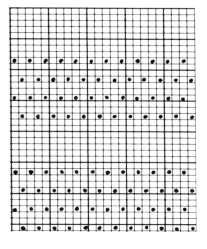

SQUARES, SOLIDS AND LACE

Multiples of 12/Tension 5
100% Chenille

The pattern illustrated uses solid colour, but this design is ideal to experiment with, using a number of colours and textures. The obvious development is to introduce a new colour every time the squares change. A more adventurous development would be to introduce 2 rows of another coloured yarn on the last row and first row of where the squares change. Textured yarns would also add to the richness of the surface of the fabric.

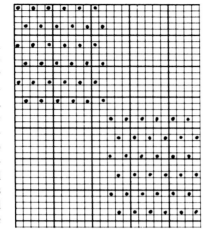

LACE TRELLIS

Multiples of 6/Tension 5-6
100% Cotton perle

An all-over lace which gives a wonderful three-dimensional effect when knitted in cotton on a tight tension. If you desire a softer look, use wool or acrylic. Rather wonderful effects can be obtained by introducing stripes of colour, and it is an ideal pattern on which to get rid of all those ends of cones and balls of yarn.

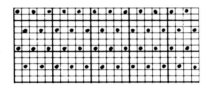

LADDER LACE

Multiples of 12/Tension 8
100% Cotton gimp

This simple lace stitch is included because, while pretty in itself, it can be developed into a wonderfully textured design by threading tape yarn or cord through the ladder holes. You could also use fabric paints to decorate the wide flat vertical stripes of stocking stitch.

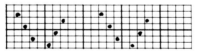

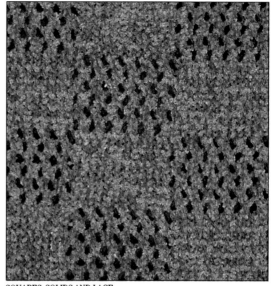

SQUARES, SOLIDS AND LACE

LACE TRELLIS

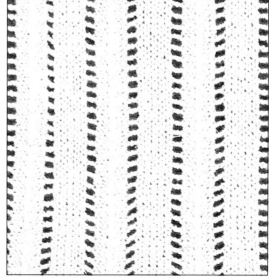

LADDER LACE

CRISS-CROSS LACE STRIPE

This is a very easy design to experiment with as can be seen in Versions I, II and III. Version III keeps the same design, but repeats it across the knitting differently by changing the pattern. See graph.

Versions I and II
Multiples of 4/Tension 6
100% Acrylic

If this design is knitted in wool or cotton, a more raised effect is achieved.

Version III
Multiples of 12/Tension 9
100% Rayon

This could be made more interesting by changing the colour in the 6 stocking stitch rows. Another colouring suggestion is:
*4 rows col A.
 6 rows col B.
 4 rows col A.
 6 rows col C.
 4 rows col A.
 6 rows col D.
 Repeat from *.

Obviously there are many variations of this open to experiment until a pleasing colouring is found. Try mixing matt yarns (wool) with shiny (rayon) ones.

The contrast can be attractive and adds texture to the construction.

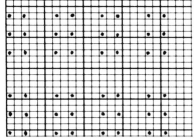
Version I

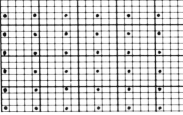
Version II

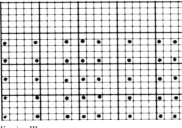
Version III

LARGE HORSESHOE

Multiples of 12/Tension 4-5
100% Cotton

This is a development of Horseshoe Stitch on page 32. It has been enlarged and wide areas of stocking stitch placed between the lace. You can develop this stitch by altering the number of needles, knitting more stocking stitch between the lace and between repeats of the lace. If you place the lace repeats close together, you can thread fancy yarn through to give added decoration.

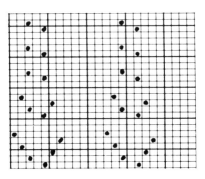

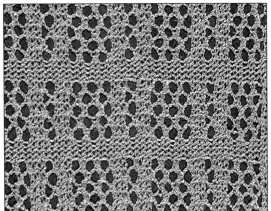

CRISS-CROSS LACE STRIPE   Top: Version 1   Above: Version III

LARGE HORSESHOE

Right: CRISS-CROSS LACE STRIPE Version II

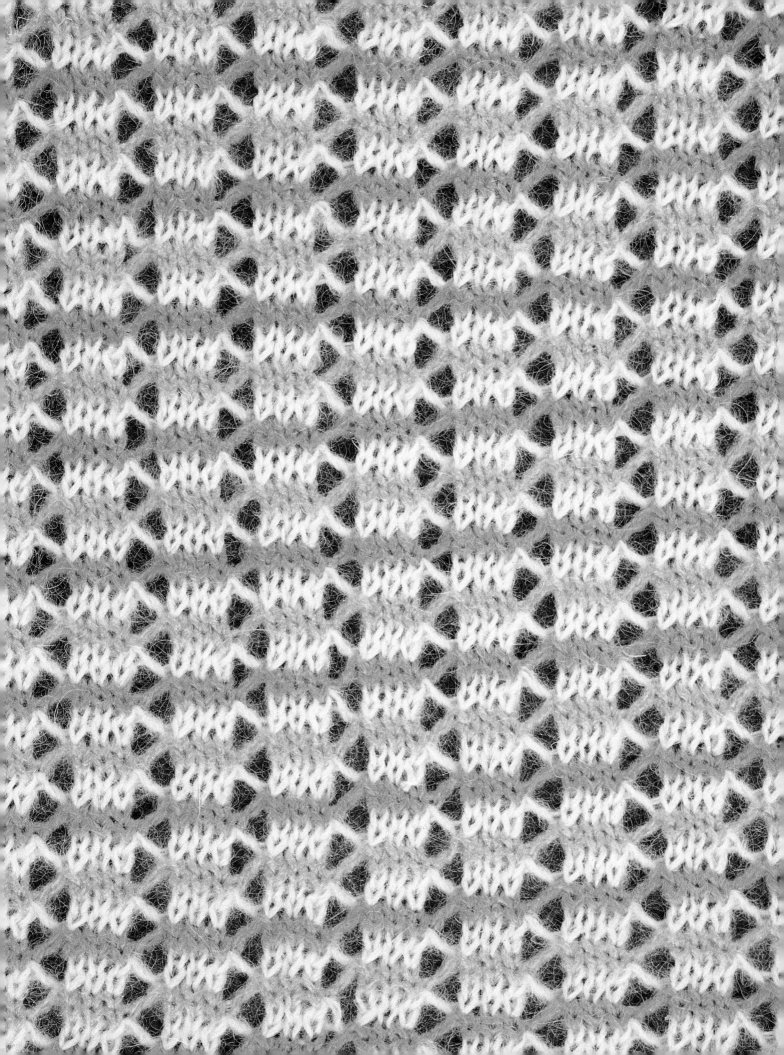

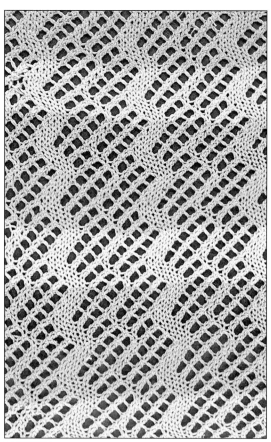

LACE TWIST

LACE TWIST

Multiples of 12/Tension 6
100% Cotton perle

This pattern is very attractive and offers many opportunities to experiment with different yarns and colours.

Although only 3 colours are used in the swatch illustrated, many more could be added. Textured yarns would also add interest. For the more adventurous knitter, adding plain rows between repeats of the design as it is in the graph could be tried.

Colour sequence:
*12 rows col A (lilac).
 12 rows col B (pink).
 12 rows col C (green).
 Repeat from *.

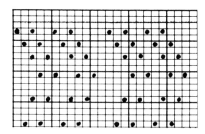

LACE SQUARES AND CABLES

Multiples of 12/Tension 7
100% Cotton

Row 1: Start lace. Miss 7 sts. Cable 4 sts crossing 2 sts at L over 2 sts at R. Miss 1 st. Repeat across row. K 1 row.
Rows 2, 3 and 4: K.
Row 5: work as row 1.
Rows 6, 7 and 8: K. Stop lace.
Rows 9, 10, 11, 12, 13 and 14: K.
Row 15: *miss 1 st, cable 4 sts crossing 2 sts at L over 2 sts at R. Miss 1 st. Repeat across row. K 1 row.
Rows 16, 17 and 18: K.

Row 19: work as row 15.
Rows 20, 21, 22, 23 and 24: K. Return to row 1.

Added colour could enliven this design. A simple development would be not to cable between the lace but to add a second colour or textured yarn instead.

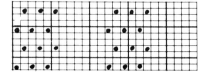

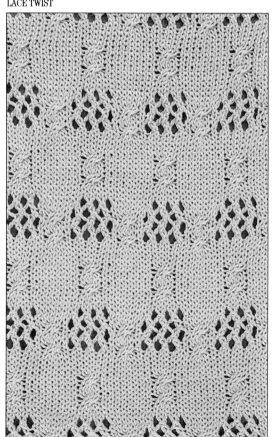

LACE SQUARES AND CABLES

FLORETS

Multiples of 12/Tension 6
100% Rayon multicolour

Version I

Solid multicoloured rayon
Set for lace, insert PC and K.
Not illustrated.

Version II

Colour sequence:
*2 rows col A (silver) feeder A.
 4 rows col B (lilac).
 2 rows col A.
 4 rows col C (peach).
 2 rows col A.
 4 rows col D (grey).
 2 rows col A.
 4 rows col E (pink).
 Repeat from *.

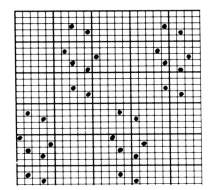

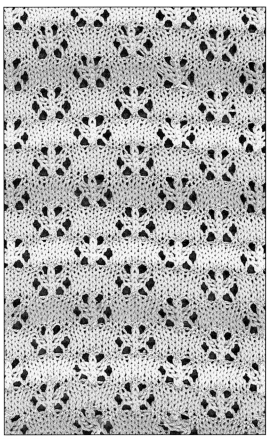

FLORETS Version II

LACED AND BRUSHED STRIPES
manual transfer lace

Multiples of any even number/
Tension 7
Lambswool and tweed cotton/
acrylic

*K 4 rows col A (cream tweed).
Make holes by transferring every
alternate st to the next needle. K 4
rows. Repeat, making holes, but
this time transfer the alternate sts
to those in row 1. This will stagger
the holes. K 4 rows. This forms
the pattern sequence.
Change to col B (orange
lambswool), K 14 rows.
Change to col A and repeat pattern sequence.

You can make the design any
proportion you wish by extending or reducing the number of
rows in each repeat.
Sequence as illustrated is:

*K 4 rows col A then transfer alternate sts across needle bed.
K 4 rows col A.
K 14 rows col B.
K 4 rows col A then transfer alternate sts across needle bed, repeat
twice, remembering to stagger
transferred sts in 2nd repeat as instructed above.
K 4 rows col A.
K 16 rows col B.
K 4 rows col A then transfer alternate sts across needle bed, repeat
3 times.
K 4 rows col A.
K 8 rows col B.
K 4 rows col A then transfer alternate sts across needle bed.
K 4 rows col A.
K 16 rows col B.
Repeat from *.

When the swatch is complete,
brush the lambswool plain
stripes with a teasel or dog brush
to bring up the pile. Illustrated is
one stripe which has not been
brushed so you can see the difference. Also illustrated is an idea
for decorating the plain pile
stripes with embroidery.

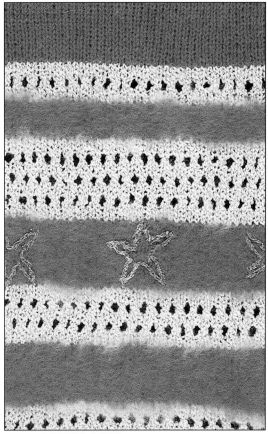

LACED AND BRUSHED STRIPES

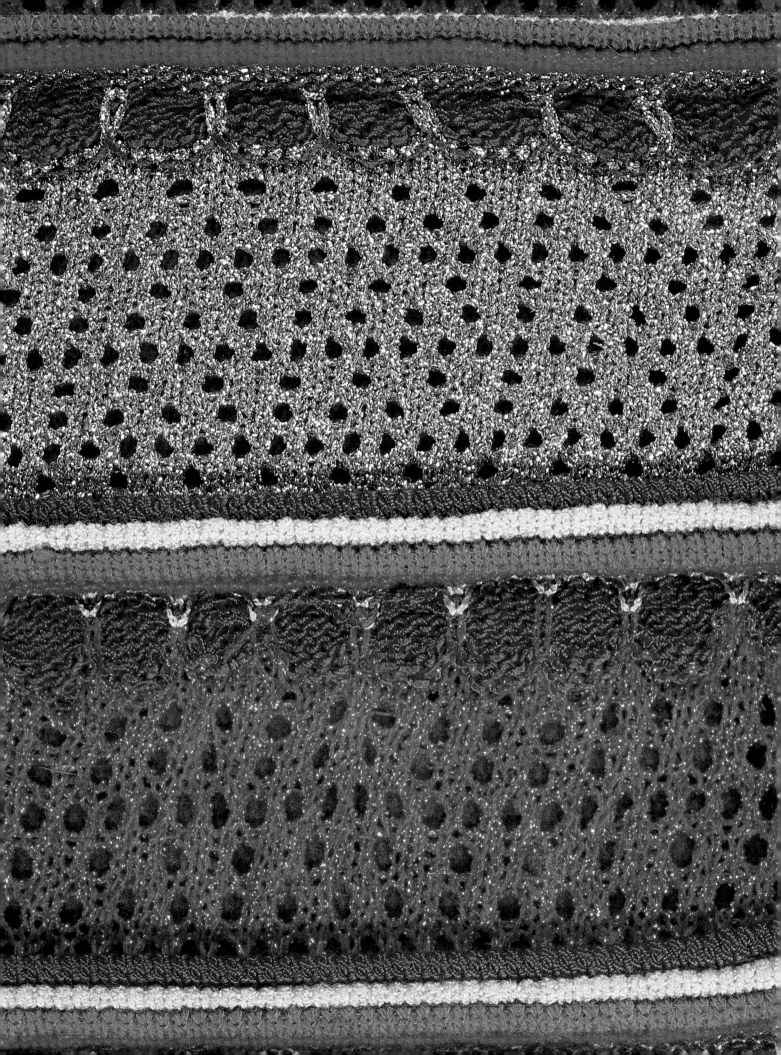

RIDGED LACE

Multiples of 6/Tension 8
Lurex cord and cotton

*Set for lace and K 1 repeat of PC in col A (red lurex).

Turn knitting around by using a garter bar or by hand and hook back onto needles. Set for normal knitting. K 10 rows col B (blue). Pick up every 6th st from last row of col A.

K 5 rows col C (yellow). Turn knitting around as before using garter bar or by hand.

**K 8 rows col A. Pick up loops from 1st row of col A and replace on needles to form pleat. Repeat from ** 3 more times using col D (green), col C and finally col B. Repeat this whole sequence from *.

This forms the complete repeat as illustrated.

Each time the punchcard is used for the lace use col A and col E (gold) alternately.

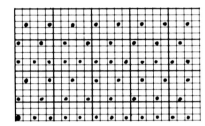

ELIZABETHAN BROCADE
manual stitch transfer

Multiples of 14/Tension 8 and 6
Cotton chenille; lurex cord

*K 1 row col A (rust chenille) T8. Start transferring sts as in graph, knitting 2 rows between each. Stop when you reach the centre of the diamond as marked.

Set for partial knitting, change to col B (gold). Push all needles except the 5 centre needles in every diamond into HP. Change to T6 and K 6 rows. Change to normal knitting col A, T8 and continue with transfer pattern. Partial knitting takes place every 12 rows. Repeat from *.

This pattern could easily be translated onto a punchcard.

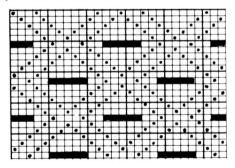

DIAMOND LADDER

Multiples of 12/Tension 5
100% Cotton

This design is quite open, the lace pattern having two distinct elements – diamonds and a ladder construction. For this pattern, it is important that none of the needles used is strained. In knitting the ladder, which is built up of hole upon hole, any malfunction of the needle will result in the holes being distorted.

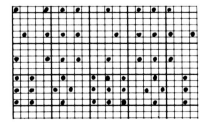

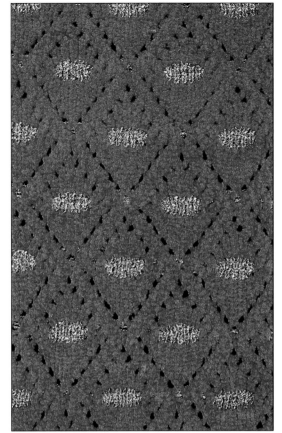

ELIZABETHAN BROCADE

Left: RIDGED LACE

DIAMOND LADDER

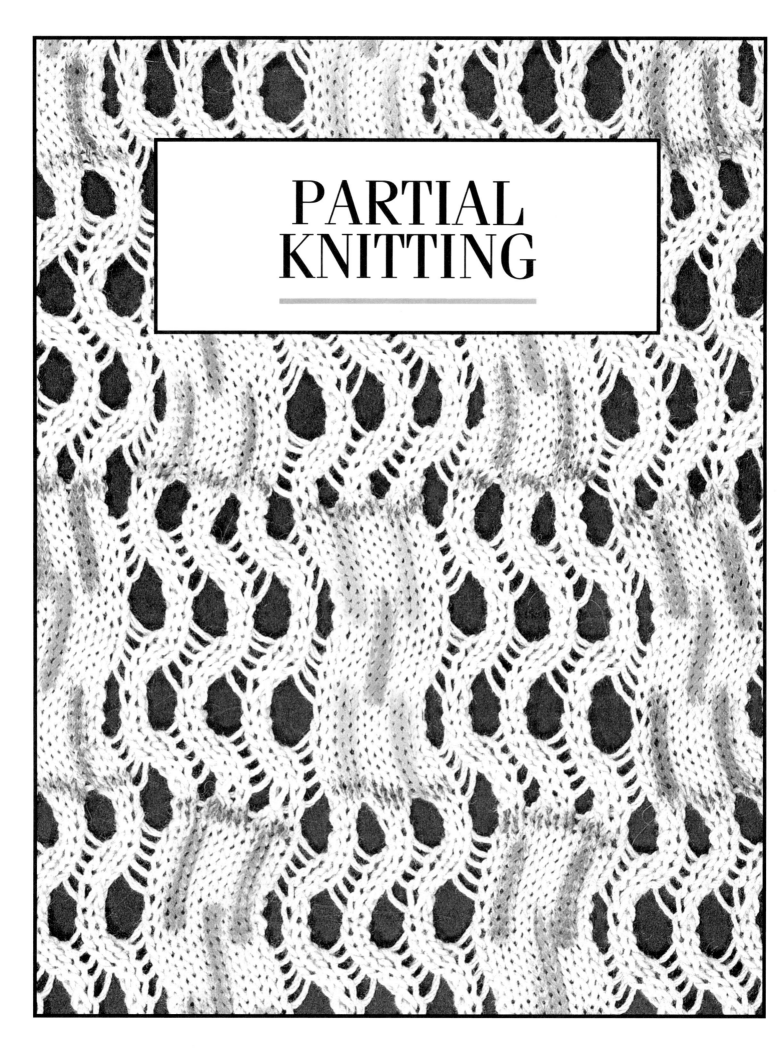

PARTIAL
KNITTING

As the name suggests, this technique involves knitting some stitches in a row, while others are held on the needles. The patterning needles are all selected manually, whereas in most other techniques the needles to be knitted on are selected by punchcard or electronic graph. Manual selection is made by pushing selected needles into the working position and others into the non-working position. Since the grouping of selected needles can be altered at will, this method offers an infinite variety of patterning.

To knit the designs illustrated, the machine controls have to be set for 'partial knitting'. On some machines, this control is marked 'holding cam' or 'returning' – it may be necessary for you to refer to your own machine manual. What all these controls have in common is that they allow all the needles left in the hold position not to be knitted when the yarn carriage is taken across the knitting bed – the stitches are simply held. When these needles are needed to knit, they are pushed into the normal upper working position. The order in which needles are held or knitted determines the pattern. Many of the patterns may appear complicated, but once the technique of partial knitting has been understood, all that is needed is a little care and patience. When starting, it is advantageous to use yarns which knit easily; the best are wool, acrylic and cotton. Rayon and slippery yarns should not be tried until the knitter has gained some experience as the end stitches can slip from the needles. With experience, any yarn can be used, with changes of colour and yarn in the middle of individual rows.

Many unique textural effects and surfaces can be produced by partial knitting, particularly raised patterns and random bobbles. Unusual lace fabrics can also be knitted. The designs illustrated show a variety of ideas using different yarns, all of which can be developed and changed. The appearance of many of the designs is radically altered by using different textured yarns and by changing the tension. A loose tension can give a delicate cobweb-like surface; a tight tension gives a raised three-dimensional quality. Changing the tension in one pattern at regular intervals produces interesting textures in addition to the normal patterning.

Partial knitting can be used in shaping garments and a good example is the flare or dart. The heel of a sock is also shaped by the partial-knitting technique. The decorative qualities and possibilities explored here show how this adaptable technique enables the knitter to produce unusual and exciting fabrics.

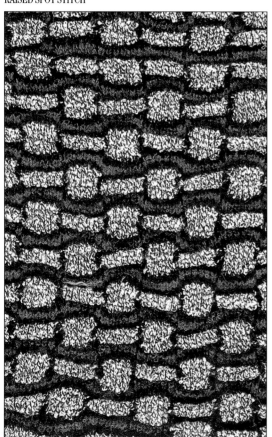

RAISED SPOT STITCH

RAISED SPOT STITCH

Multiples of 15/Tension 6
Shetland wool and 4-ply acrylic

Carriage on R, K 10 rows col A (white), all needles UWP. Change to col B (multicolour).
*Push all needles into HP, except 1st 15 on R, K 1 row. Push all needles except 1st 6 on L into HP, K 7 rows, carriage on R. Using a transfer tool, pick up the 2nd loop down between working and non-working stitches and hook this loop onto the outside needle of the set of 6 being knitted. Do this both sides, which forms the raised spot. Push next 15 needles on L into UWP, K 1 row. Push all needles into HP except 6 on extreme L, K 7 rows. Pick up outside loops as before and place on outside needles. Repeat this sequence from *. On arriving at extreme L of knitting, change yarn to col A and K 9 rows with all needles in UWP. Carriage on L, change yarn to col B and begin again. The repeat from L to R begins as follows. All needles in HP except 1st 21, K 1 row. Push all needles into HP except last 6 needles on R, K 7 rows. Carriage on L, pick up loops as already described, push next 15 needles into UWP, K 1 row. Push all needles except 6 on R into HP, K 7 rows. Now carry on knitting as before, going from L to R.

The first sequence every time you knit from L to R is altered from the usual 15 needles to 23. It is simple to reposition the raised spots so that they fall correctly into a half-drop pattern. Once you have mastered this stitch, you can try repositioning the spots in more elaborate patterns of your own. Many exciting designs can be knitted by manipulating this stitch.

RIPPLE SEERSUCKER STITCH

Needle set-out 111111·111111·111111·111111 (have an even number of sets of 6).
Tension 6 (for soft standard yarns a firm, but not tight, tension is needed.
Shetland wool and multicolour 4-ply.

Pattern repeat:
*Carriage on R.
  K 2 rows col A (black Shetland).
  K 2 rows col B (multicolour 4-ply).
  K 2 rows col A.
  Change to col C (tweed yarn).
Push all needles except 1st set of 6 into HP, K 8 rows. Pick up the 2nd loop down between stitches being worked and those being held, and hook this loop onto the outside needle of the set being worked on. Do this on both sides of the set of needles. Push 2nd set of 6 needles into UWP, K 1 row, carriage on L. Push 1st set of needles into HP, K 7 rows, carriage on R. Push next set of 6 needles into UWP, K 1 row. Push RH set of needles into HP, K 7 rows, carriage on R. Pick up loops as before between working and non-working stitches and hook onto outside needles. Note that this process is only carried out on alternate sets of needles. This is important as it gives the ripple seersucker effect. Continue this sequence across knitting until the extreme L of work is reached. Repeat from *, but this time working from L to R.

RIPPLE SEERSUCKER STITCH

BLACK AND WHITE PILLAR STITCH

Needle set-out 111·111·111·
Tension 8
Shetland wool and cotton gimp

Pattern repeat:
*K 4 rows col A (black).
K 2 rows col B (white).
K 4 rows col A.
Carriage on R, push all needles except 1st set of 3 into HP. Change yarn to col B, K 10 rows. Push 2nd set of 3 needles into UWP and K 1 row. Stop carriage on L and push 1st set of 3 needles into HP. K 9 rows ending with carriage on R. Push 3rd set of 3 needles into UWP, K 1 row. Push RH set of 3 needles into HP, K 9 rows, carriage on R. Repeat across knitting ending with carriage on L. Repeat from *, but this time knitting from L to R. At the end of this sequence the carriage is on the extreme R. The above forms one complete pattern.

BLACK AND WHITE PILLAR STITCH

RIB AND RIPPLE STITCH

Needle set-out 1111·1111·1111· (have an even number of sets of 4).
Tension 7
Shetland wool

Pattern repeat:
*All needles in UWP.
K 2 rows col A (pink).
K 2 rows col B (orange).
K 6 rows col C (purple).
K 2 rows col A (alternate repeats col D (yellow)).
K 6 rows col C.
K 2 rows col B.
K 2 rows col A, change to col D.
Carriage on R, push all needles except 1st set of 4 into HP, K 8 rows. Push 2nd set of 4 needles into UWP and K 1 row, carriage on L. Push 1st set of needles into HP, K 7 rows. (NB: after 6th row and before 7th row, pick up the second loop down between stitch being knitted and those not being knitted and hook it onto the outside needle of the set of 4. Do this on both sides of the set of 4 needles being knitted.) Carriage on R, push next set of 4 needles into UWP, K 1 row. Push set of needles on R into HP, K 7 rows, carriage on R. Repeat this across the bed of knitting. Note that loops are only picked up on alternate sets of needles, which gives the ripple effect. The carriage is on the extreme L. Now repeat from *, this time working from L to R.

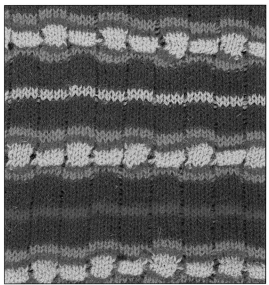

RIB AND RIPPLE STITCH

DIAMOND

Multiples of 10/Tension 6
Standard Shetland wool and 4-ply acrylic

All needles in work, K 15 rows MC (black), carriage on R. Change to col B. Push 1st 14 needles into HP, leave next 2 needles in WP and push all other needles into HP. K 1 row, then introduce 1 needle to WP on opposite side to the carriage every row until 10 needles are working. Push all 10 needles into HP and then leaving a gap of 14 needles in HP, introduce next 2 needles to WP and repeat, until you have worked across the whole knitting. K 4 rows. To complete diamonds, push 1st 10 needles into HP, next 10 to WP and remainder of needles to HP. K 1 row, then push into HP 1 needle on opposite side to carriage. K 1 row and repeat until only 2 sts remain. Push into HP and, counting 10 needles, push the next 10 into WP and repeat until you have worked across the whole knitting. Change colour to MC and K 15 rows. This is the whole repeat.

The diamonds can be worked all in one colour or as shown here in 4 different colours.

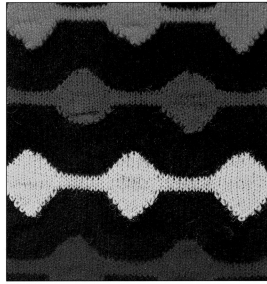

DIAMOND

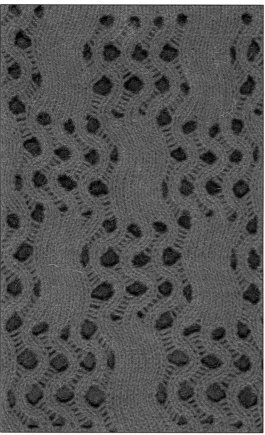

CHECKED WAVES Version I

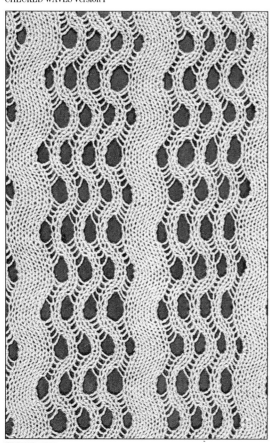

WAVY STRIPE

CHECKED WAVES

Multiples of 18/Tension 6
Shetland wool

Version I

1st pattern row:
K 8 rows plain, then counting from the R, transfer 9th, 12th, 15th and 18th sts in every block of 18 needles.

Push empty needles into NWP. Push all needles except 1st 8 into HP, K 4 rows. Push into WP the next group of 2 needles, K 4 rows. Carriage on R, push into WP the next group of 2 needles, K 1 row. Push 1st group of 8 into HP, K 3 rows. Push next group of 2 into WP, K 1 row. Push group on L into HP, K 3 rows; push next group of 8 into WP, K 1 row; push last group of 2 on R into HP, K 4 rows; push next group of 2 into WP, K 1 row. Push last group of 2 on R into HP, K 3 rows. This forms the repeat. Remember the last set of needles, whether 8 or 2, are knitted on their own.
Carriage on L.

2nd pattern row:
As 1st pattern row, but working from L to R and reading R for L.

3rd pattern row:
Work as 1st pattern row.

4th pattern row:
Push all needles into WP, including those in NWP. Counting from the R, transfer the 3rd, 6th, 9th and 18th stitches onto adjacent needle in every block of 18 needles. Carriage on L, K 4 rows on 1st group of 2 needles, push next set of 2 needles into WP, K 4 rows. Carriage on L, push into WP next group of 2 needles, K 1 row; push 1st group of 2 into HP, K 3 rows; push next group of 8 into WP, K 1 row; push last group of 2 on L into HP, K 3 rows; push next group of 2 into WP, K 1 row; push last group of 2 on L into HP, K 3 rows; push next group of 2 into WP, K 1 row; push last group of 8 on L into HP, K 3 rows.

Version II

This is worked exactly as Version I, but in 100% natural cotton. When complete, it is decorated with fabric crayons. Use your own drawn design rather than copy mine. You can also change the needle set-out to make the squares larger or smaller, allowing more scope for crayon decoration afterwards.

WAVY STRIPE

Multiples of 16 + 6/Tension 5
Cotton

1st pattern row:
Carriage on R.
K 10 rows, transfer to the R the 7th, 10th, 13th and 16th sts in every block of 16 needles. Push all empty needles into NWP. Push all needles except 1st 6 on R into HP, K 4 rows. Push into WP next group of 2 needles, K 4 rows. Carriage on R. Push into WP next group of 2 needles. . K 1 row. Push 1st group of 6 into HP and K 3 rows. Push next group of 2 into WP, K 1 row. Push group on R into HP, K 3 rows. Push next group of into WP, K 1 row. Push last group of 2 on R into HP, K 4 rows. Push next group of 2 into WP, K 1 row. Push last group of 2 on R into HP, K 3 rows. This forms the pattern. Remember that the last set of needles will be knitted on their own.

2nd pattern row:
Work as for 1st pattern row, but work from L to R and read R for L and L for R.

These 2 pattern rows form the design illustrated.

Right: CHECKED WAVES Version II

MULTICOLOURED RAISED SPOT STITCH

RAISED LOOP STITCH

MULTICOLOURED RAISED SPOT STITCH

Tension 6
4-ply wool
This stitch is really a 5-spot repeat.

K 4 rows col A (navy blue), carriage on R. Push all needles into HP except 1st set of needles to form spot. K 10 rows col B, break off yarn, then lift loop between outside stitch of those which are knitting and those not knitting, and hook it over outside needle. Do this at either end of 4 just knitted. Push all needles into HP except next 4 to be knitted; put col C into carriage which should be on R of needles in WP. Make sure yarn end is lying over the needles in HP and falls over those down in front of 4 needles ready to knit. This is important to ensure it is picked up easily by 1st needle in knitting position. K 10 rows and proceed as before. Continue until you have completed the sets of 4 needles forming the 1st row of spots across your swatch. Change yarn. Carriage now on L, K 4 rows. Push all needles into HP, take carriage to R of knitting, push into work 1st 4 needles of 2nd row of spots as on graph and proceed as before. Continue this sequence for each row of spots, always K 4 rows between col A until entire 5-row repeat is completed. Then start the whole sequence forming the total repeat over again until you have the length of knitting required. A little care should be taken when knitting the 1st row of col A each time as this is the row which picks up and knits in the loops which form the raised spot.

This pattern can also be worked in just 2 colours or, as illustrated, a textured yarn could be introduced for either the main colour or spot.

RAISED LOOP STITCH

Multiples of 11/Tension 5.5
Cotton crêpe yarn and 4-ply multicoloured acrylic

*K 10 rows col A (rust cotton crêpe), all needles in UWP. Push all needles except first 11 into HP. Change to col B (multicoloured acrylic) and K 1 row ending with the carriage on L. Push all needles except 1st 3 on L into HP, K 7 rows. The carriage is now back on R. This sequence is now repeated across the bed of knitting. On reaching the L, change yarn to col A and repeat from *. When you start the repeat from the L, the first selection of needles is 16, not 11. This is to form a half-drop repeat or stagger the loops being knitted – ie, 16 needles in UWP, K 1 row in col B. Push all needles except last 3 on R into HP, K 7 rows. Push 11 needles to UWP, K 1 row. Push all needles except last 3 on R into HP, K 7 rows. Repeat as before.

When the knitting is complete, the fabric can be used just as it comes off the machine, or it can be decorated by threading ribbon or yarn through the loops. The illustration shows one way of doing this, but you could invent your own. Once you have mastered the stitch, you could begin by placing the knitted loops in different sequences and so create many more designs. This technique can be used to great effect on selected areas of a sweater.

SOFT SEERSUCKER STITCH

Needle set-out 1111·1111·1111· (have an even number of sets of 4 needles)
4-ply wool

K 2 rows col A (orange) all needles in work.
K 2 rows col B (yellow) all needles in work. Carriage on R. Change to col C (green). Push all sets of 4 needles into HP except 1st set on right. K 6 rows. Push next 2 sets of 4 needles into WP, K 1 row. Push the 2 sets of 4 needles on R into HP, K 6 rows, carriage on R. Push next 2 sets of needles on L into WP, K 1 row. Push the 2 sets of needles on R into HP, K 6 rows. This is the repeat. Continue across the knitting until the carriage is on L.
Push all needles into WP.
K 2 rows col B.
K 2 rows col A. Change to col C. Push all needles into HP except 1st set of 4, K 6 rows. This is the start of the repeat, except this time you work across the machine from L to R. Note the colour changes when all needles are knitting, between partial-knitting sequences col A and col B change positions each repeat (see illustration).

SOFT SEERSUCKER STITCH

MULTIPLE WAVE

Multiples of 3/Tension 8.5
Cotton and rayon chenille

1st pattern row:
K 10 rows col A (red). Transfer every 3rd stitch onto needle on R and push the empty needle out of work. *Carriage on R, push all needles except 1st 2 on R into HP and K 4 rows. Push 2nd pair of 2 into WP, K 4 rows. Carriage on R. Push next 2 needles into WP, K 1 row. Push 1st pair on R into HP, K 3 rows. Carriage on R. Push next 2 needles on L into WP, K 1 row and push 1st pair of needles on R into HP, K 3 rows. This forms the pattern. Continue across the whole bed of knitting.* Carriage on L.

2nd pattern row:
Work as for 1st pattern row, but use col B (blue) and work from L to R and read R for L and L for R. These 2 rows form the pattern illustrated.

MULTIPLE WAVE

WHITE PILLARS

Multiples of 4/Tension 7
4-ply Acrylic

Carriage on R.
K 8 rows col A (blue). Push all needles except 1st 4 into HP, change to col B (white) and K 1 row, carriage on L. Push 1st 2 needles into HP, K 7 rows, carriage on R. Push 4 more needles into WP, K 1 row, carriage on L. Push the 4 needles on R into HP, K 7 rows. This forms the repeat, leaving carriage on L. Repeat from L as before, starting with 8 rows of col A.

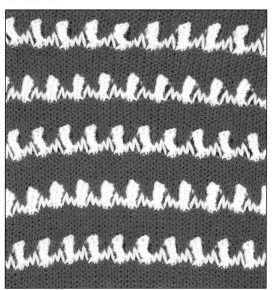
WHITE PILLARS

BOBBLES AND BEADS

Tension 4
Fine acrylic

K 20 rows col A (green).
*Set for partial knitting. Push every alternate set of 3 needles into HP across your knitting. K 6 rows col B (red), T 5.
Set for normal knitting. K 6 rows col A, T 4.
Set for partial knitting. Push 1st set of 3 needles and every alternate set of 3 needles into HP.
K 6 rows col C (yellow), T 4.
Set for normal knitting. K 6 rows col B, T 5.
Repeat this sequence from * once more, using different colours for partial knitting (see illustration).
Set for partial knitting. Push every alternate set of 3 needles into HP until there are 6 sets of 3, then push 18 needles into HP and repeat across your knitting.

K 7 rows, alternating col B and col C, T 4.
Return to normal knitting. K 6 rows col B, T 5.
Set for partial knitting. Push 1st 36 needles into HP, then leave 3 in WP and next 3 in HP. Repeat over next 18 needles, then repeat this whole sequence across knitting.
K 7 rows, alternating col D (gold) and col E (blue).
Return to normal knitting. K 10 rows col A.
Set for partial knitting, pushing every alternate set of 3 needles into HP. K 8 rows. Set for normal knitting. K 8 rows col A, T 5.

Beads can be knitted in at this point or sewn on afterwards. Knit in the beads, spaced every 4th st. K 2 rows col D, T 5. Knit in beads spaced every 8th st. K 5 rows of col D. Repeat from start of pattern.

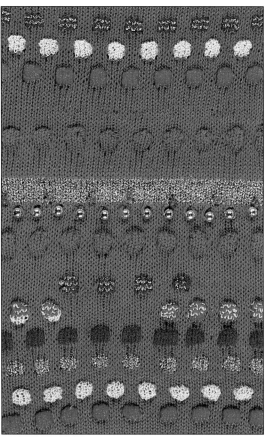

BOBBLES AND BEADS

WHITE FLAPS

Pattern divisible by 16 + 10/
Tension 7
4-ply Cotton gimp and 4-ply equivalent of loop yarn

K 8 rows col A (black), carriage on R. Push all needles except 1st 16 into HP. K 1 row col B (white). Push 1st 10 needles on R into HP, carriage on L. K 11 rows, carriage on R. Push next 16 needles on L into WP, K 1 row. Now pick up loops of the last row of col A and hook these onto the needles directly above in WP. This forms fold. Carriage on L, push 16 needles on R into HP and K 11 rows on the 6 needles in WP. This is the

repeat. When carriage arrives at L of knitting and all folds are complete, change colour to col A and K 8 rows. Starting from the L, the whole sequence is repeated, but to stagger folds, start the repeat from L as follows. Change to col B, push all needles into HP except 1st 8 and K 1 row. Push 1st 2 needles into HP, K 11 rows. Push next 11 needles into WP, K 1 row. Hook up loops as before on folds, carriage on R. Push 16 needles on L into HP and K 11 rows. Repeat this across knitting. These 2 repeats, R to L and L to R, form the complete pattern.

WHITE FLAPS

WAVES

Multiples of 10/Tension 5.5
Cotton perle yarn and rayon

Carriage on L, K 15 rows col A (pink cotton). Push all needles into HP, except 1st 2. Change to col B (rayon), K 10 rows, then push next 2 needles into WP. K 1 row, then push 1st 2 needles into HP, K 9 rows, carriage on R. Push next 2 needles on L into WP, K 1 row; push the 2 needles on R into HP, K 9 rows. This forms the repeat for partial knitting, except that every alternate set of 5 knitted strips is hooked up to form a loop. To do this, pick up loops of the last row of col A and hook them over the needles directly above. Start with the 1st set of 5 needles on R. At the end of the repeat, K 15 rows col A, carriage now on R. Repeat the whole sequence once more. To create a staggered effect, start hooking loops on the 2nd set of 5 pairs of needles. This forms the total repeat illustrated.

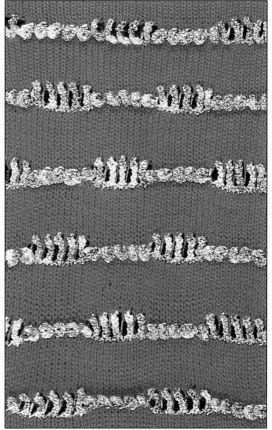

WAVES

WHITE WATER

Multiples of 3/Tension 4
Lurex twist yarn

K 4 rows col A (gold), 2 rows col B (silver), 4 rows col A, transfer every 3rd stitch onto needle on L and push empty needles into NWP. Work complete repeat of 1st pattern row from Multiple Wave pattern (p53) for White Water in col B. Carriage on L, push all needles in HP and NWP into WP and K 4 rows col A, 2 rows col B, 4 rows col A. Transfer every 3rd stitch to needle on R and push empty needles into NWP. K 2nd pattern row of Multiple Wave pattern. This forms the total design illustrated.

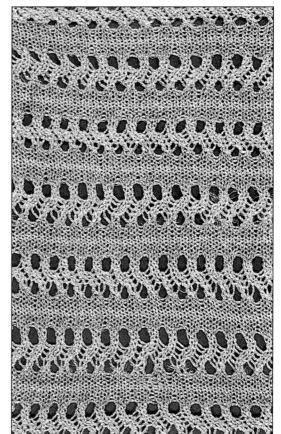

WHITE WATER

TRIANGULAR POCKETS

Multiples of 24/Tension 7
100% Cotton

Cast on 24sts. * K 36 rows to form a square. Hook the LH st of the 1st row of knitting onto the RH st on the top row. Hook on the rest of the sts and K 1 row; this seals the triangle. K 35 rows and cast off.* Repeat from * to * until you have as many pieces as you require. Fold triangles over squares to form triangular pockets as illustrated. Sew squares together any way you find attractive.

To make black cones, cast on 5 sts, K 10 rows. Fold over to make a small triangle as in the main sample, hooking sts onto needles in work. K 1 row to seal and cast off. Turn triangle inside out and sew onto finished sample as illustrated.

To finish off, decorate triangles with Swiss darning, as shown. Follow the graphs provided using 3 colours. This fabric can be left as it is now or objects can be sewn into the triangular pockets, such as flowers or figures as illustrated.

TRIANGULAR POCKETS

DOTS AND CORDS

Multiples of 12/Tension 9
100% Cotton chenille

**K 8 rows col A (navy blue). Push 1st 8 needles into NWP. Leave the next 4 needles in WP and repeat this sequence across the knitting.

Switch carriage to partial knitting and change to col B (maroon). K 6 rows. Return to normal knitting and col A. K 8 rows. Push the 1st 2 needles into NWP. *Leave the next 4 in WP. Push the next 8 into NWP and repeat from * across the knitting.

Set for partial knitting and K 6 rows in col B. Return to normal knitting and col A and K 16 rows. Repeat from **.

The design illustrated is completed by chain stitching around the dots. Invent your own pattern of chain stitching – many variations are possible. Using a 3rd colour for the chain stitch could add more interest.

CROSS-OVER

Multiples of 6/Tension 6
Shetland wool

K 10 rows col A (pink). Carriage on R. Push all needles except 1st 3 on R into HP. K 10 rows col B (black). Push these into HP and next 3 needles on L into WP. K 10 rows col C (yellow). Repeat this across knitting. To form cross, with transfer tools, pick up 3 sts col B and 3 sts col C and cross R 3 over L 3. Repeat this with each set of 6 needles. Now K 10 rows col A.

The repeats are all the same except that on alternate repeats of the partial knitting, start with col C, not col B.

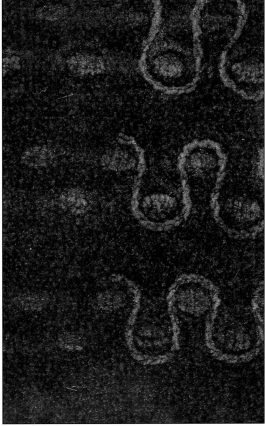

DOTS AND CORDS

Left: CROSS-OVER

JACQUARD WITH RIPPLES AND FRINGES

Multiples of 24/Tension 7
100% Acrylic, straight and looped yarns

K 8 rows col A (purple).
*Set for Fair Isle, insert PC. K 14 rows, col B (black) feeder A; col C (green) feeder B.
Remove PC and set for normal knitting.
K 10 rows col D (orange loop).
Pick up loops of 1st row col D on needles to form a ridge or pleat.
K 4 rows col B.
Set for partial knitting. Push 1st 6 needles into HP, miss 5 and push next 6 into HP. Repeat this across knitting.
K 10 rows col E (blue). Set for normal knitting.
K 4 rows col B.
K 1 row col D. Pick up loops from 1st orange ridge and replace on needles except where blue bobbles appear.
K 10 rows col D, then pick up 1st row of sts as before to form a ridge. K 1 row col D.
K 15 rows col A, then with garter bar or by hand, turn knitting around.
With a ruler held close to and under the needles, lay 2 or 3 ends together over each alternate needle, taking the yarns down the back of the ruler, under it and up in front of the ruler, before laying the yarns over the next alternate needle. This forms a large loop. Continue this across the knitting.
K 4 rows col A.
Turn knitting round again using a garter bar or by hand.
Repeat from *.

When swatch is complete, cut loops to make a fringe. The thickness of this will depend on how many ends of the yarns you decide to loop around the needles and ruler.

If you want a more random design, you can reverse the pattern or change the sequence of partial knitting and colours.

Almost anything will work provided you do not knit more than 10 rows between any pattern. Try your own combination based on the repeat set out here.

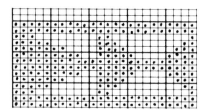

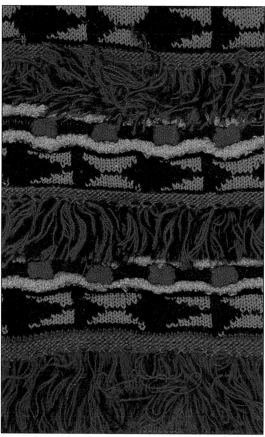

JACQUARD WITH RIPPLES AND FRINGES

MILLED SQUARES

Multiples of 12/Tension 8
Lambswool and gold lurex thread

**K 10 rows alternating col A (cream lambswool) with col B (gold lurex thread) every row.
*Change to partial knitting. Push 1st 6 needles on left into NWP. Leave next 6 needles in WP and repeat across knitting. K 1 row col A. Change back to normal knitting. K 1 row col B. Repeat this sequence from * 10 times in all, then repeat from **. This forms the pattern. It is possible to complete the partial knitting sequence, then change the tension to 6, which gives an attractive distortion when the swatch is finished.

The sample as illustrated was finished by being put in a standard coloured wash (automatic washing-machine). The milling or felting which takes place adds real interest and softness to the design. Embroidery was added around odd shapes using a fancy yarn. This enriches the surface. This design could be knitted as a jacquard, but the lovely 'tweed' background would be lost.

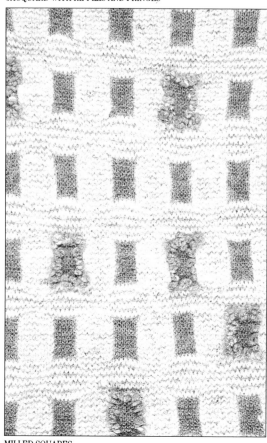

MILLED SQUARES

TWISTED DOTS AND DASHES

Multiples of 16/Tension 7
Wool gimp and 4-ply wool

Knit 6 rows col A (dark green), * change to col B (orange). K 1 row, then set for partial knitting. Counting from the L, push the following needles into HP, 1, 2, 7 and 8 in every repeat of 16 across the knitting. Change to col C (white), K 6 rows. Push all needles into WP and set for normal knitting. K 1 row col B. K 6 rows col A. To knit design illustrated, repeat from * 6 times.

Set for Fair Isle. K 6 rows col A feeder A, col C feeder B. With 2 pronged transfer tools, pick up last 2 sts of col A and the 2 sts of col C and cross them from L to R and R to L to form cable. Continue across the knitting on every set of 8 needles. This is repeated every 6 rows, but on every alternate repeat the cabling is reversed – ie, R to L and L to R. This gives the cables the curly look. After 4 repeats of the punchcard and cables, set for normal knitting and K 6 rows col A. K 1 repeat from * to *. K 6 rows col A. Repeat from ** to ** 4 times. This gives you the design illustrated, but there are many other possible combinations of these 2 sts which you can use to design your own patterns. Remember to try fancy yarns and your own colours.

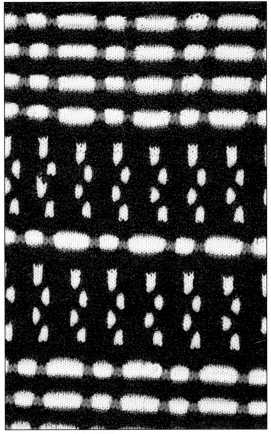

TWISTED DOTS AND DASHES

PEBBLE WALL

Multiples of 15/Tension 6
Shetland wool and rayon gimp

Push all needles except 1st 6 on R into HP. K 6 rows then push next set of 3 needles into WP. K 1 row, now push 1st set of 6 needles into HP. K 7 rows, carriage on R. Push 2nd set of 3 needles into WP. K 1 row. Push 1st set of 3 needles on R into HP. K 7 rows. *Push next block of 6 needles into WP. K 1 row. Push set of 3 needles on R into HP. K 7 rows. Push next set of 3 needles into WP. K 1 row. Now push 1st set of 6 needles into HP. K 7 rows, carriage on R. Push next set of 3 needles in WP. K 1 row. Push 1st set of 3 needles on R into HP. K 7 rows. Repeat from *.

To knit from L to R across the needle bed simply reverse instructions or, if you wish, take the carriage off the L side of the machine and reset it on the R, then follow the same instructions as just completed.

Alternatively, for a raised effect, pick up the loops of the last row of col A and hook these onto needles directly above on all sets of 3 needles before pushing them into HP each time they are knitted.

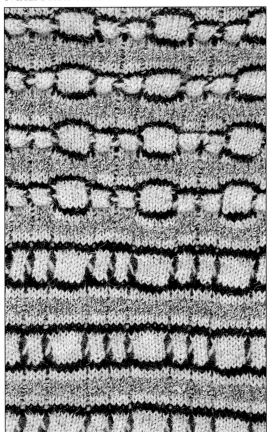

PEBBLE WALL

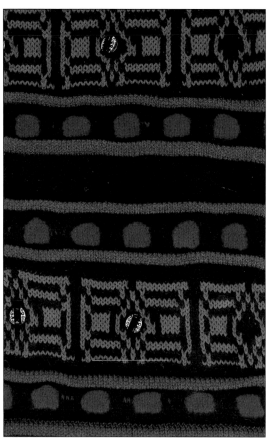

JACQUARD AND TUCK

JACQUARD AND TUCK

Multiples of 24/Tension 4
100% Acrylic

*K 14 rows col A (black). K 9 rows col B (burgundy). Pick up loops of 1st row of col B onto needles in work. This forms a pleat. K 1 row col B. K 6 rows col A. Set for partial knitting and T 2. Push every alternate set of 5 needles into HP. K 10 rows col C (blue).

Set for normal knitting. T 4, K 6 rows col A. K 9 rows col B. Pick up loops of 1st row of col B and replace on needles in work. This forms a pleat. K 1 row col B. K 4 rows col A.

Set for Fair Isle, insert PC and K col A feeder A; col D (green) feeder B (K 20 rows).

Set for normal knitting. K 4 rows col A. K 9 rows col B and hook up as before to form pleat. K 1 row col B. K 6 rows col A.

Set for partial knitting, then push every alternate set of 5 needles into HP and K 10 rows col C (blue), T 2.

Return carriage to normal knitting, T 4, K 6 rows col A. K 9 rows col B and hook up as before to form pleat. Repeat from *.

To add interest to this pattern, buttons or beads can be sewn onto the centre of the jacquard pattern, as illustrated.

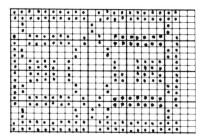

OTTOMAN TUCK

Multiples of 14/Tension 7
100% Wool

K 10 rows col A (orange). *Set for partial knitting. Push needles 1 and 2 in every set of 8 into HP, repeat across the work. Change to col B (white), K 6 rows. Set for normal knitting and col A, K 4 rows.

**Set for partial knitting and push needles 1, 2, 7 and 8 of every set of 16 into HP across the work. Change to col B, K 6 rows.

Set for normal knitting, K 6 rows in col A. Repeat from ** 3 times.

***K 12 rows col A. To create ridge, pick up loops from every 4th st on the 4th row down and hook onto the needles in work. Repeat from *** 3 times. The total repeat is from *.

This design can be developed by inventive use of colour and textured yarns.

By using rayon as col B and wool as col A, then milling the sample, an interesting fabric with an unusual textured surface is produced. For milling, see introduction to tuck stitch.

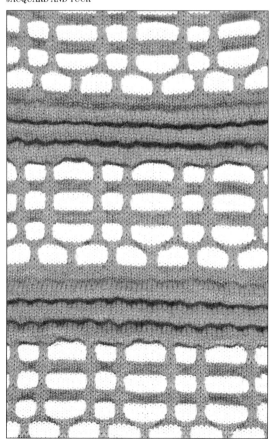

OTTOMAN TUCK

FRINGED BORDER

Multiples of 24/Tension 7
Wool and looped acrylic

K 4 rows col A (black), then transfer every 6th st onto adjacent needle at L to make holes. K 4 rows col A. K 8 rows col B (purple). Pick up every 3rd st, from 1st row of col B and hook onto needles in work. K 3 rows col A.

Set for partial knitting, push needles 1, 2, 3 and 4 into HP. Leave 8 in work and repeat across knitting. K 10 rows col C (green).

Set for normal knitting. K 3 rows col A. K 8 rows col B. Pick up every 3rd stitch from 1st row of col B and hook onto needles in work. K 5 rows col A.

*Transfer 1st st in every set of 3 onto adjacent needle at L to make holes.

K 3 rows col A. Repeat from * but transfer 2nd st in every set of 3 this time.

K 8 rows col A.

Insert PC 1 and set for Fair Isle. Col A feeder A. Col D (orange) feeder B. K 1 repeat, then return to normal knitting. K 26 rows col A.

Using garter bar or by hand, turn knitting around. The front is now facing you. K 1 row col A. Taking a ruler, hold it close to and under the needle bed and with col B lay the yarn over the 1st needle, then down behind the ruler, under it and up the front of the ruler. This forms a loop around the ruler.

Now repeat this sequence right across the knitting using alternate needles only.

K 4 rows col A. Remove ruler carefully and cut loops to create fringe. Set for tuck stitch, insert PC 2 and K in col A to complete swatch.

To finish off sample, take a few ends of black yarn and thread them through the holes made at the start of the knitting. This will create a fringe.

PC2

PC1

FRINGED BORDER

LOOPED STRIPES

Tension 5
Acrylic loop yarn and rayon tape

*K 16 rows col A (acrylic loop yarn). Push alternate needles forward and, holding a ruler close to and under the needle bed, take yarn over the 1st needle, down and round and up the ruler forming a loop and then over the next needle. Repeat across knitting on all selected needles using col B (rayon tape).

K 1 row col A, cast off. You now have a strip of knitting with loops on it. Put to one side. Cast on same amount of sts as before in col A. Now pick up the long loops of the strip of knitting you have just completed and place on alternate needles.

Repeat from * being careful to hold down the piece hooked on for the 1st row. Make sure the same side of the knitting is always facing you when it is hooked on.

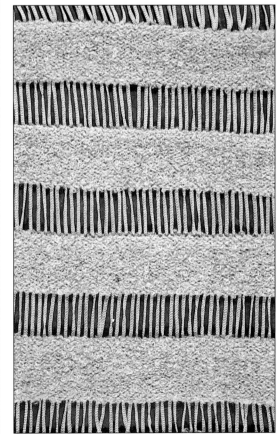

LOOPED STRIPES

JACQUARD (FAIR ISLE)

Jacquard and Fair Isle are two terms in machine knitting used to describe the same stitch structure, namely where two different coloured or textured yarns are knitted in one row. Because I have worked in the Shetland Islands and know how strongly the knitters there feel about the arbitrary use of the term Fair Isle, I use it only for multicoloured designs which are indigenous or based on traditional Fair Isle patterns. The term jacquard I use to refer to multicolour figurative designs generally. Some machine manufacturers, however, use the term Fair Isle to refer to all knitting in which two or more colours are knitted in one row; to knit the designs in this section you will have to set your machine for Fair Isle patterning if you own one of these machines. It is possible to use up to four colours in any one row in machine knitting, but the graphing of such patterning is not easy and is beyond the scope of this book.

I have tried to present here a wide variety of designs to appeal to many tastes, and all the patterns can be developed and personalised by experimenting with yarns and colour. Jacquard designs can also be changed by inserting strips of plain knitting between repeats, or more radically by introducing stripes of textured stitches between stripes of jacquard. Another device for adding interest is the needle-out technique. This is achieved by designing a jacquard pattern which allows for odd needles in a prearranged position to be pushed out of work. When knitted, ladder effects run vertically up the fabric which can then be used for decorative purposes such as threading ribbon through. There are a number of examples of such designs in this section. All the patterns illustrated are contained easily on one graph or punchcard but it is possible, by joining punchcards, to have much longer repeats which can be extremely interesting and give the appearance of great complexity. This is something worth thinking about and exploring.

It is interesting to see how beautiful and unusual shapes are enhanced by the interchange of light and dark colours. Colour work often brings out the best in a designer's ingenuity and it is well worth spending time experimenting with different colours and tones in one design before deciding what the final colour combination should be.

The balance of a design can sometimes be altered completely by changing or reversing the colour tones. A good example of this is the Peacocks design (page 73). Here, in one swatch, the birds come forward on the fabric to appear very three-dimensional. By changing the colour tones and so the colour balance, this three-dimensional appearance is lost and the birds become much less important in the second version. It is worth trying this technique of colour usage on other designs, to create your own illusions and effects.

Try to use these jacquard designs as a starting point only, from which to experiment and develop your own unique designs.

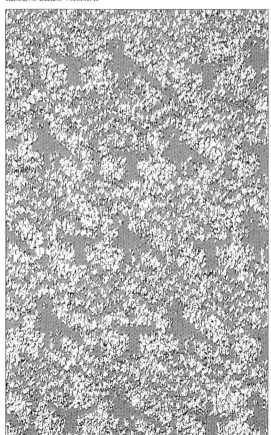

KISSING BIRDS

Multiples of 24/Tension 8
100% Wool

In Version I the odd rows allow the knitter to introduce colour in such a way as to produce a colourful complex-looking fabric, while in Version II the more classic look is obtained by restricting the colours to just three. By changing the colour sequences many variations can be produced.

Version I

Colour sequence:
13 rows col A (navy) feeder A; col B (blue) feeder B.
6 rows col C (rust) feeder A; col D (purple) feeder B.
3 rows col B feeder A; col A feeder B.
2 rows col D feeder A; col E (khaki) feeder B.
3 rows col B feeder A; col A feeder B.
6 rows col C feeder A; col D feeder B.

Version II

Colour sequence:
MC (white) constant in feeder A.
13 rows col A (blue) feeder B.
6 rows col B (grey) feeder B.
3 rows col A feeder B.
2 rows col B feeder B.
3 rows col A feeder B.
6 rows col B feeder B.

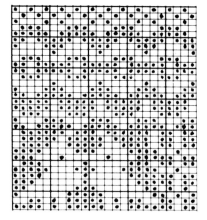

KISSING BIRDS Version II

BIRD BATH

Multiples of 24/Tension 8
Shetland and gimp yarn

This design works very well in just two colours, but the surface and pattern are both enhanced and become much richer if one yarn is changed to a tweed fancy yarn. The composition of this yarn really does not matter – it is the look which the textured yarn creates that is all-important.

Col A (black-and-white gimp) feeder A.
Col B (orange) feeder B.

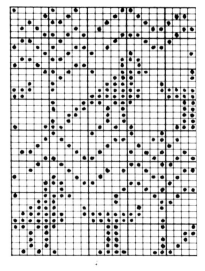

BIRD BATH

Right: KISSING BIRDS Version I

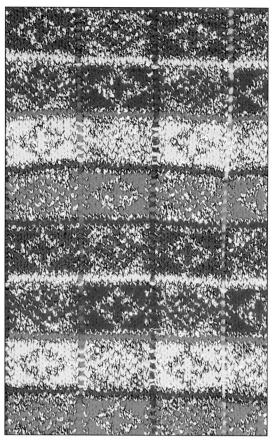

DIAMOND AND CROSS

DIAMOND AND CROSS

Multiples of 24/Tension 7
Shetland and gimp wool tweed

First get the pattern working as a normal jacquard.
Push into NWP the 1st and 13th needle in every repeat of 24 needles. These non-working needles will create a ladder effect.

*K 1 row col A (green) feeder A only.
K 11 rows col B (tweed) feeder A; col D (yellow) feeder B.
K 1 row col C (red) feeder A only.
K 11 rows col B (tweed) feeder A; col E (blue) feeder B.
K 1 row col D (yellow) feeder A only.
K 11 rows col B feeder A; col A feeder B.
K 1 row col E feeder A only.
K 11 rows col B feeder A; col C feeder B.
Repeat from *.

When swatch is complete, 2 strands of the Shetland coloured yarns are threaded through alternate loops of the ladder formed by non-working needles. Use a bodkin for this and follow the colour sequence green, red, yellow, blue repeat. This will give an attractive over check to the design.
On the graph, NWP is indicated by ⟨.

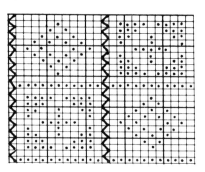

NEEDLE-OUT CHECKS

Tension 8

These two designs are not strictly jacquard although they look like it. They are very simple and many variations can be worked on them.

Version I
Needle set-out ·111111·111111·

*K 10 rows col A (navy wool).
K 2 rows col B (pink looped mohair).
Repeat from *.

When the pattern is finished take 2 ends of the looped mohair and thread these through the ladders left where the needles were out of action. This forms the check.

Version II
Needle set-out ·1111·1111·1111·

K 8 rows col A (white wool).
K 2 rows col B (dark green wool).
When pattern is complete take 2 ends of col B and thread them through the ladder left where the needles were out of action. This forms the check.

This pattern can be changed radically by putting more needles out of action, enabling more ladders to be made and different colours and yarns to be threaded through them.
Not illustrated.

NEDDLE-OUT CHECKS Version I

TAPESTRY

Multiples of 24/Tension 8
Shetland and tweed wool

This design is based on Renaissance fabrics and the crimped tweed yarn is used to give the surface a rich texture. This pattern can be interpreted in many different combinations of colours and it would also be good to run an elasticated yarn in with one of the yarns used. Such a combination of yarns would give a seersucker fabric.

Col A (maroon Shetland) feeder A.
Col B (tweed wool) feeder B.

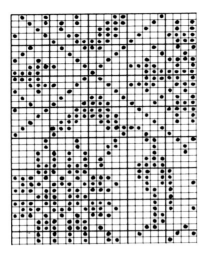

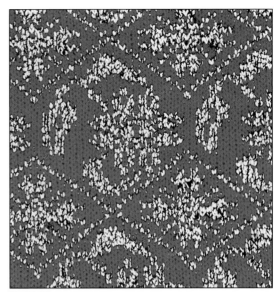

TAPESTRY

ISLAM

Multiples of 12/Tension 8
100% Shetland

This geometric design was inspired by small pieces of Turkish rugs. With this in mind experiment with colour. The diamond shapes do not overlap which makes it possible to change colours on the last and first rows of these shapes without cutting across them.

Col A (green) feeder A.
Col B (rust) feeder B.

Experiment by changing the colour in feeder B every 8 rows, or by changing the colour in feeder B on rows 7, 8, 15 and 26. This means you have to knit single rows but the resulting design will be worth the extra effort.

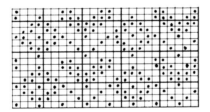

ISLAM

TRAM LINES

Multiples of 2 and 4/Tension 8
100% Wool

These two simple stripes are extremely useful designs to use in conjunction with other patterns. They work equally well in subtle or contrasting colours. Textured yarns would add interest.

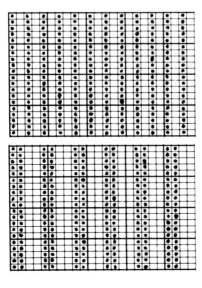

TRAM LINES

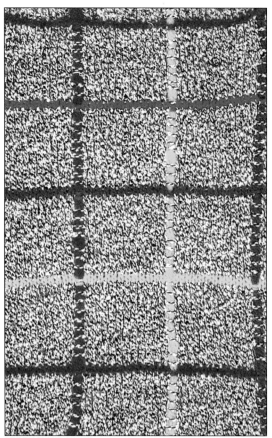

MULTICOLOUR CHECK

TILES

MANGY DOG

Multiples of 24/Tension 8
Wool with tweed gimp yarn

This design is great fun to experiment on with colour and textured yarns. Many different types of dog can be created simply by alterating its interpretation.

Colour sequence:
*3 rows col A (black) feeder A;
    col B (multicolour) feeder B.
  24 rows col A feeder A; col C
    (brown/white tweed) feeder B.
  Repeat from *.

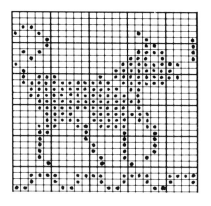

MULTICOLOUR CHECK

Needle set out
    111111111111·111111111111·
Tension 7
100% Shetland and gimp wool tweed

*K 14 rows col A (tweed).
 K 2 rows col B (blue).
 K 14 rows col A.
 K 2 rows col C (yellow).
 K 14 rows col A.
 K 2 rows col D (green).
 K 14 rows col A.
 K 2 rows col E (red).
 Repeat from *.

When knitting is complete take the fabric from the machine and with a bodkin thread 6 strands together of the red yarn through alternate loops of the ladder made by non-working needles. Repeat this through each ladder using each colour in the order knitted, ie, red, blue, yellow, green, repeat. This design can be knitted in any combination and fancy yarns could be substituted for the colour Shetland used here.

TILES

Multiples of 24/Tension 7-8
100% Shetland

This tile design is actually two designs combined, one a leaf pattern and one a geometric. Separate them to produce a totally new tile design.

Think about real decorative tiles and their shiny surface, which may suggest different yarns to use and experiment with.

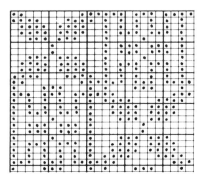

Right: MANGY DOG

BIRD'S-EYE STRIPE

ELONGATED GEOMETRIC

BIRD'S-EYE STRIPE

Multiples of 8/Tension 8
Black wool and multicolour acrylic

This is a very simple stripe which looks good in many different 2 colour combinations. Close tones used together give a lovely tweedy effect. Experiment by changing colours every 4th and 6th row.

ELONGATED GEOMETRIC

Multiples of 24/Tension 7
Cotton tweed and acrylic

Two punchcards are needed joined together.
Set carriage for Fair Isle.
Knit following colour sequence:
*K 22 rows col A (tweed) feeder A;
    col B (navy) feeder B.
  K 2 rows col A feeder A only.
  K 8 rows col A feeder A; col C
    (burgundy) feeder B.
  K 2 rows col A feeder A only.
  K 54 rows col A feeder A; col B
    feeder B.
  K 2 rows col A feeder A only.
  K 14 rows col A feeder A; col C
    feeder B.
  K 2 rows col A feeder A only.
  Repeat from *.

Because of the arrangement of pattern within this design, colour changes can be worked easily without upsetting the balance. Invent alternative colourways, changing the yarns at the plain rows.

FLOWER IN LOZENGE

Multiples of 24/Tension 8
Cotton and acrylic

Version I

The combination of black acrylic with cream cotton works very dramatically in this design giving a strong crisp image.

Col A (black) feeder A.
Col B (cream) feeder B.

Version II

Here the strong design line has been softened and gives a totally different appearance. This altering of a design by the use of colour and textured yarn can be used to great advantage in many stitches and jacquards.

Col A (orange cotton) feeder A.
Col B (black-and-white cotton) feeder B.

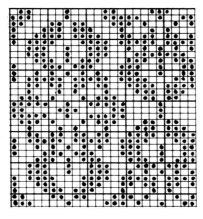

FLOWER IN LOZENGE   Top: Version I   Above: Version II

ABSTRACT FLOWER

Version I

Multiples of 12/Tension 8
100% Shetland

This is knitted in 2 colours and could be made more interesting by introducing a textured or tweed yarn. Not illustrated.

Version II

Multiples of 12/Tension 6
100% Cotton

This is knitted in 6 colours.

Colour sequence:
MC (navy) constant in feeder A.
*25 rows col B (rust) feeder B.
 5 rows col C (yellow) feeder B.
 25 rows col D (red) feeder B.
 5 rows col E (blue) feeder B.
 25 rows col F (green) feeder B.
 5 rows col C (yellow) feeder B.
 Repeat from *.

By keeping the main colour constant and using 5 colours for the flowers, the colour repeat becomes quite long giving the illusion of an extremely rich complicated design. This method of colouring could be tried on other designs.

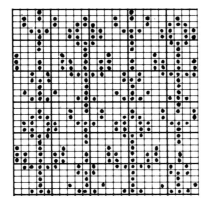

ABSTRACT FLOWER Version II

DANCING SNOWMAN

Multiples of 24/Tension 8
Black wool and white looped mohair and rayon mixture

This is a humorous design and although it has been coloured and knitted here as one would expect for a snowman, the design lends itself to other colourings. Bright primary colours look good as they exaggerate the fun of the pattern.

PEACOCKS

PEACOCKS

Multiples of 24/Tension 8
100% Shetland

These two interpretations of peacocks illustrate how different a design can look by changing the position of the darkest colour. The whole balance of the design changes. In this instance both work well, but often when changing the colour balance one combination works well, while the other is rather weak.

In the yellow and space-dyed yarn version the space-dyed yarn has given the pattern an almost Persian carpet look. This could be further exploited.

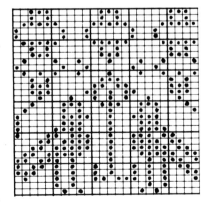

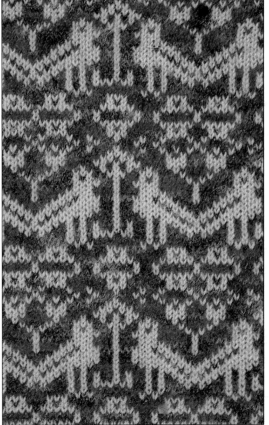

Left: DANCING SNOWMAN

PEACOCKS

DRAGON

DRAGON

Multiples of 24/Tension 5-6
Acrylic and rayon

The dragon is great fun and I have used fun colours to emphasise this. This design could be knitted simply in two colours but the yellow looped rayon gives an added element of richness and lifts the colours.

Colour sequence:
*6 rows col A (blue) feeder A; col B (yellow) feeder B.
36 rows col A feeder A; col C (red) feeder B.
Repeat from *.

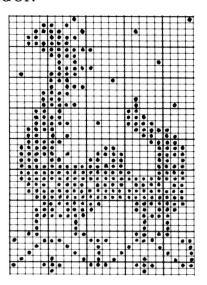

RARE RABBIT

Multiples of 24/Tension 6
Wool/rayon mixture, wool mohair and snarl yarn

Rare Rabbit shows just one of the many combinations of yarns and textures which can be used for this design. Try out your own ideas. If you use textured yarn on the rabbit, give it a little brush with a teasel brush to exaggerate the texture. For children really bright colours used in an irregular sequence could look great.

Colour sequence:
*3 rows col A (blue) feeder A; col B (green) feeder B.

24 rows col A feeder A; col C (white) feeder B.
Repeat from *.

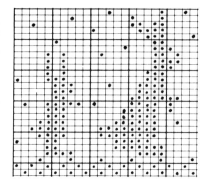

RARE RABBIT

SPACE INVADER

Multiples of 12/Tension 7
100% Shetland

A subtle design image made to appear complex by clever colouring. For the less adventurous the pattern can be knitted in just two colours. The pattern lends itself to many interpretations and colour changes.

Colour sequence:
*10 rows col A (brown) feeder A; col B (green) feeder B.
2 rows col C (pink) feeder A; col D (green) feeder B.
2 rows col E (blue) feeder A; col B (green) feeder B.
4 rows col A feeder A; col B feeder B.

4 rows col B feeder A; col E feeder B.
2 rows col C feeder A; col A feeder B.
4 rows col B feeder A; col E feeder B.
Repeat from *.

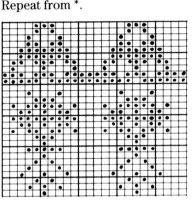

SPACE INVADER

ROBOT

Multiples of 24/Tension 6-7
Shetland and multicolour acrylic

This is a fun design and the colours used exaggerate it. The colour sequence changes quite often but the resulting fabric is worth the effort.

The robot man would look good if knitted in metallic or lurex yarns. Once again experiment and create your own interpretation of the pattern.

Colour sequence:
*8 rows col A (black) feeder A; col B (blue) feeder B. X
2 rows col A feeder A; col C (red) feeder B.
26 rows col A feeder A; col D (multicolour) feeder B.
8 rows col A feeder A; col B feeder B. X
2 rows col A feeder A; col C feeder B.*

Next complete repeat substitute col E (green) for col B where marked X.
These 2 colour repeats form the total colour repeat as illustrated.

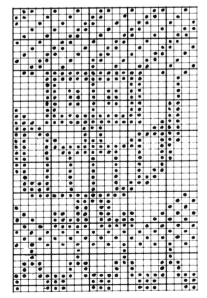

ROBOT

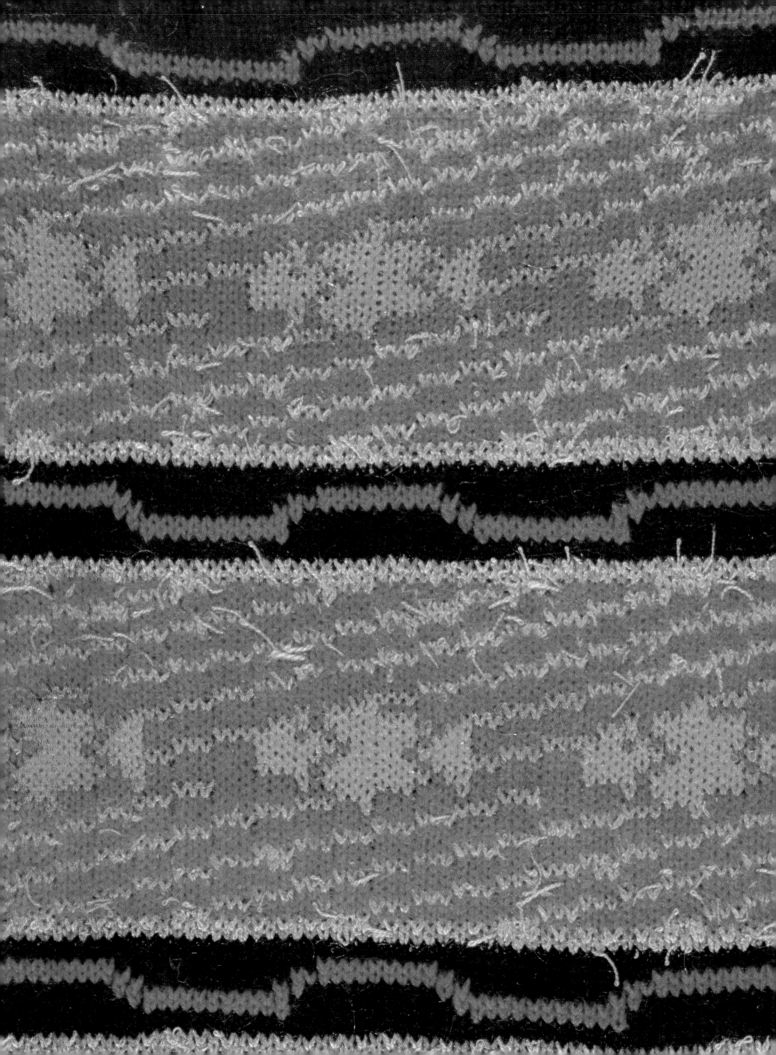

GOLDEN CARP

Version I (orange fish)
Multiples of 24/Tension 5-6
Acrylic with rayon snarl yarn

*2 rows col A (green) feeder A;
col B (orange) feeder B.
9 rows col C (black) feeder A;
col D (blue) feeder B.
2 rows col A feeder A; col B
feeder B.
11 rows col D feeder A; col A
feeder B.
11 rows col D feeder A; col B
feeder B.
11 rows col D feeder A; col A
feeder B.
Repeat from *.

Version II (golden fish)
Multiples of 24/use appropriate
tension for the yarn thickness,
slightly loose
Rayon and cotton yarns

*2 rows col A (white) feeder A;
col B (yellow) feeder B.
9 rows col C (pink) feeder A;
col D (blue) feeder B.
2 rows col A feeder A; col B
feeder B.

11 rows col D feeder A; col A
feeder B.
11 rows col D feeder A; col B
feeder B.
11 rows col D feeder A; col A
feeder B.
Repeat from *.

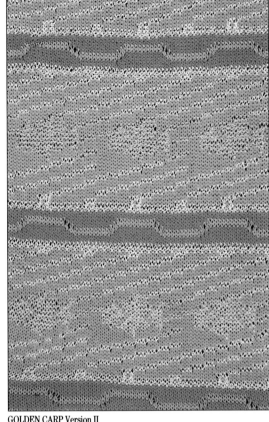

GOLDEN CARP Version II

INSPIRED FAIR ISLE

Multiples of 24/Tension 8

This is such a versatile design
that 2 versions are illustrated to
encourage experimentation with
colour and texture.

Version I
Black wool and cream cotton
gimp.

Version II
100% Wool

Colour sequence:
*7 rows col A (white) feeder A;
col B (khaki) feeder B.
5 rows col A feeder A; col C
(grey) feeder B.
5 rows col A feeder A; col D
(navy) feeder B.
5 rows col A feeder A; col B
feeder B.

6 rows col A feeder A; col D
feeder B.
5 rows col A feeder A; col C
feeder B.
Repeat from *.

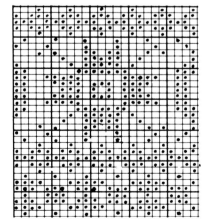

INSPIRED FAIR ISLE   Top: Version I   Above: Version II

Left: GOLDEN CARP Version I

DIAMOND STRIPE

DIAMOND STRIPE

Multiples of 24/Tension 7
Acrylic and multicolour rayon

Set machine for Fair Isle and knit one repeat of the pattern using MC (navy-blue) in feeder A and multicolour in feeder B.

On the first row of the second repeat transfer stitches 10 and 22 of each repeat of 24 needles across your knitting onto adjacent needles at R. Push all empty needles into NWP. Refer to graph and note these are the central stitches at the bottom of the two chevrons which form part of the pattern. When swatch is complete ladders are formed where needles have been out of work. Using a bodkin thread through alternate loops rayon tape or fancy yarn.

On some machines, eg Brother, the effect of taking needles out can alter the stitch construction. This is illustrated on the top half of the sample. If this occurs switch the carriage from KCI to KCII and the same card will knit as illustrated in the bottom half.

If you have a machine which is confused in this way by pushing needles out of work, you can use this as a design aid on many other designs. Experiment with your machine to see what happens when needles are pushed into NWP when using punchcard patterns.

On the graph, NWP is indicated by ⌇.

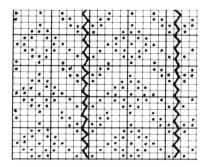

WOBBLE FLOWER

Multiples of 24/Tension 5
Rayon and cotton

K 10 rows col A (beige) T5 and lock PC.
*K 4 rows col B (gold) T8 feeder A.
Make ridged pleat by picking up loops of 1st row of col B and hooking them onto needles in work.
T5, col C (dark green) feeder A; col D (turquoise) feeder B.
Release PC. K 22 rows.
K 4 rows col B T8 feeder A and make ridged pleat as before.
T5, col A feeder A, col E (pink) feeder B.
K 12 rows.
Repeat from *.

Each time the pattern illustrated was knitted, the colour combinations were changed, but they could remain the same throughout.

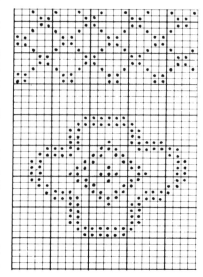

WOBBLE FLOWER

78

TRIANGLES, TUCK AND LETTERS

Multiples of 24/Tension 4
Acrylic colours; gold lurex cord

K 10 rows col A (red).
K 4 rows col B (gold).
Set carriage for partial knitting then push 1st 8 needles into HP and 2nd 8 needles into WP. Repeat this across the knitting.
K 2 rows col A.
Reset carriage for normal knitting. K 10 rows col B.
K 10 rows col A. Transfer alternate sts to adjacent needles across knitting.
K 10 rows col A. Pick up sts from 1st row col A (20 rows down). This makes a picot hem.
K 1 row col B.
K 1 row col C (navy). Repeat this sequence 5 times.
K 11 rows col C. Pick up sts from 1st row col C and replace on corresponding needles. This makes a pleat.
K 12 rows col A.
K 12 rows col D (green) and pick up sts from 1st row to form pleat as before.
K 8 rows col A.
Set carriage to Fair Isle and insert PC1. Col A feeder A; col B feeder B.
Knit one repeat then reset carriage for normal knitting.
K 15 rows col A.
*K 10 rows col E (silver and gold lurex) T2.
K 8 rows col D, T4, then pick up every 8th st from 1st row of col E and hook them onto corresponding needles.*
K 4 rows col A.
Set carriage to Fair Isle and insert PC2. Col A feeder A; col B feeder B.
K one repeat of PC.
Reset carriage for normal knitting. K 4 rows col A.

Finish swatch by knitting the sequence between * and * once more.
To finish this sample K triangles of col D and col E and sew these onto knitting as illustrated. You can also add beads for extra richness.
To make triangles cast on 12 sts and cast off one st each end of knitting every 2 rows until only one st is left. Cast off.

Once you have knitted this design you will be able to make your own patterns from different parts of it. Try rearranging the sequences of the original.

PC1

PC2

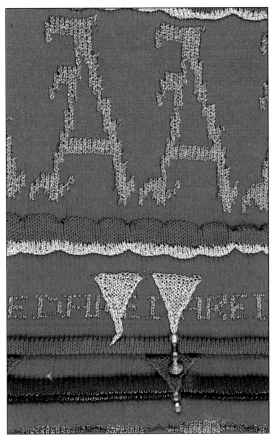

TRIANGLES, TUCK AND LETTERS

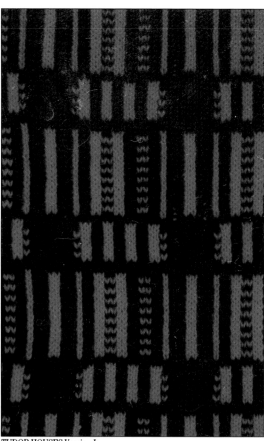

TUDOR HOUSES Version I

TUDOR HOUSES

Multiples of 24/Tension 8
100% Shetland

Version I

This design was inspired by Tudor houses.

Col A (red) feeder A.
Col B (black) feeder B.

Version II

By exchanging the dark for the light colours the design can be changed quite radically.

Colour sequence:
*6 rows col A (white loop) feeder A; col B (navy wool) feeder B.
 6 rows col B feeder A; col A feeder B.
 Repeat from *.

On the graph, NWP is indicated by ⟨.

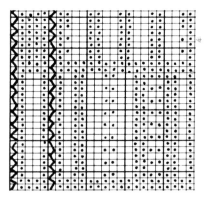

DINOSAUR

Multiples of 24/Tension 5-6
100% acrylic

This design is arranged in such a way that it is possible to change the colour in the places indicated without creating strange stripe effects. Experiment with different textured yarns and colours to create your own personal dinosaur.

Colour sequence:
*14 rows col A (purple) feeder A; col B (green) feeder B.
 8 rows col C (pink) feeder A; col D (yellow) feeder B.

4 rows col C feeder A; col B feeder B.
Repeat from *.

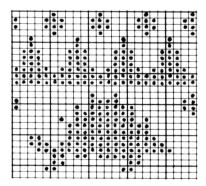

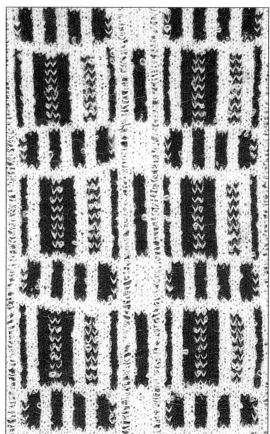

TUDOR HOUSES Version II

Right: DINOSAUR

FLOWER BORDER

RIB AND SMOCK

FLOWER BORDER

Multiples of 24/Tension 6
Linen, acrylic and lurex cord yarn

K 25 rows col A (linen).
Change to col B (gold lurex yarn).
Switch to partial knitting.
Leaving the first 5 needles on L in WP push the rest of the needles into NWP.
*K 12 rows.
Change to waste yarn, K 6 rows.
Push the 5 needles in WP into NWP. Count 20 needles along from these to R and bring next 5 needles in WP.
Repeat from *.
Repeat this sequence across knitting (ie, knitting on 5 sts with 20 sts in between in NWP).
Remove each section of partial knitting in gold lurex and push the small strip knitted through the hole between the original knitting and bring it down and round up the front of the knitting to face you. Remove waste yarn and replace sts on empty needles. This looping and replacing of the partially knitted strips will have gathered the knitting into swags. Switch back to normal knitting.
K 10 rows col B. Pick up the loops from 1st row of gold and hook onto needles in work to make a tucked pleat.
Set carriage for Fair Isle T6 col C (blue) feeder A; col D (maroon) feeder B.

K 22 rows.
Change to col E (green) feeder B and K 8 rows which completes the jacquard pattern.
Set for normal knitting and with col B in feeder A, K 10 rows at T10. Pick up loops from 1st row of col B and hook onto needles in work to make tucked pleat.
Change to col A T6 and complete swatch.
The design as it comes off the machine is very attractive but you can embellish it as illustrated by Swiss darning round the flowers in pink silk and by outlining the pink with gold thread. The central flower is also changed by Swiss darning and the whole, outlined in gold. The small border at the top of the jacquard has also been stitched round. It is not necessary to copy this exactly; be inventive!

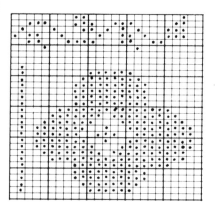

RIB AND SMOCK

Tension 8
100% Cotton chenille

This is not a jacquard, but looks like one. Set machine for normal knitting.
*K 4 rows col A (burgundy).
K 3 rows col B (navy).
Pick up sts from the first row col B and replace them on needles in work. This forms a ridged pleat.
Repeat from *.

The knitting is used on its side and smocking is made by sewing the ridged pleats together at intervals. Here a contrasting yarn is used. You could also use a multicolour yarn or a number of different colours for the smocking.

For those knitters with a double bed machine, this design could be knitted as a 1 x 3 rib and the ribs used in the same way as the ridged pleats are here.

ELASTICATED JACQUARD

Multiples of 24/Tension 6
Cotton and lurex cord

Set machine for Fair Isle and knit colour sequence as follows:
12 rows col A (green) feeder A; col B (gold cord) feeder B.
3 rows col A feeder A only.
23 rows col A feeder A; col C (navy elasticated yarn) feeder B.
2 rows col A feeder A only.
3 rows col B feeder A only.
12 rows col B feeder A; col D feeder B.
5 rows col B feeder A only.
24 rows col B feeder A; col C feeder B.
2 rows col B feeder A only.
2 rows col A feeder A only.
12 rows col A feeder A; col E (yellow) feeder B.
2 rows col A feeder A only.
23 rows col A feeder A; col B feeder B.
2 rows col A feeder A only.
2 rows col B feeder A only.
12 rows col D feeder A; col B feeder B.
4 rows col B feeder A only.
This unusual swatch could be used as part of a garment – for example the ends of sleeves or the bottom half of a sweater where the elastication would take the place of the usual welts. On the design illustrated, two of the gold swirls have been embroidered over and 2 punchcards have been joined together to allow for the length of the pattern.

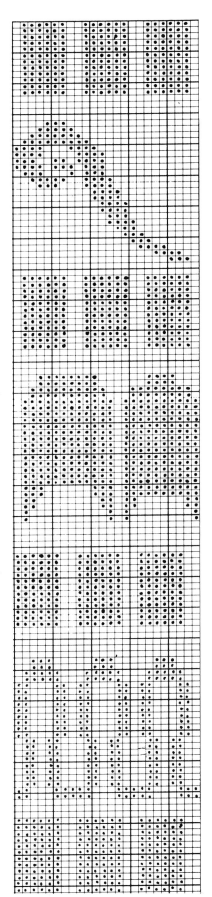

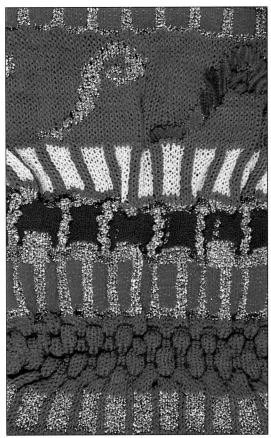

ELASTICATED JACQUARD

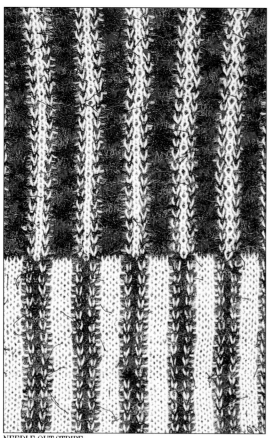

NEEDLE-OUT STRIPE

NEEDLE-OUT STRIPE

Multiples of 8/Tension 8
White mohair and wool with multicolour acrylic loop yarn

Start this pattern with all needles in work. Then transfer 4th stitch onto needle on left and transfer 8th stitch onto needle on right. Push these 2 empty needles into NWP. Repeat this on every repeat of 8 needles across your knitting. Set machine to Fair Isle and begin knitting (if using a Brother machine switch to KC II).
   The design is shown knitted in two different ways. This is achieved by changing the colours round in the feeders. This technique can be tried in other patterns to great effect.

On the graph, NWP is indicated by ₹.

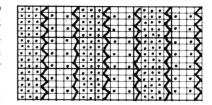

HARLEQUIN

Multiples of 24/Tension 7 and 4
Cotton and lurex

K 10 rows waste yarn, T7.
K 8 rows col A (gold lurex). Make picot by transferring every alternate st to the adjacent needle.
K 8 rows then pick up sts of 1st row col A. This gives you a picot edge.
K 5 rows col A and remove waste yarn knitting.
K 5 rows col B (red) T4.
K 5 rows col A T7.
K 5 rows col B T4.
K 6 rows col C (green). Pick up alternate sts from 1st row col C and replace needles in work. This forms a ridged pleat.
K 1 row col B.
Set carriage to Fair Isle and insert PC.
K 1 repeat of PC, col B in feeder A, col C in feeder B ending with 4 rows col B.
Set carriage for normal knitting.
*K 6 rows col D (yellow) T4. Pick up stitches of 1st row col D and replace on needles in work to form ridged pleat.
Repeat from * using col C and then col B. (There should now be 3 ridged pleats.)
K 2 rows col C.
Set carriage for Fair Isle and insert PC.
K 1 repeat of PC, col C in feeder A, col D in feeder B ending with 4 rows col C.
Set carriage for normal knitting.
**K 1 row col A T7, then transfer every alternate st by hand to adjacent needle to create eyelet.
Repeat from ** twice more.
K 5 rows col B T4.
Set carriage for partial knitting and push needles 1, 2, 3 of every set of 6 into HP.
K 6 rows col C.
Set carriage for normal knitting.
K 10 rows col B. Cast off.
To knit triangles cast on 12 sts and K 6 rows, dec 1 st at each side of work. Repeat this sequence until you are left with 1 st. Cast off.
Sew triangles onto fabric to create the design illustrated. Add beads if you wish. This design can be used as a yoke or border on a garment.

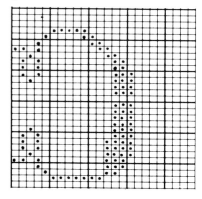

Right: HARLEQUIN

LEAF GRID

LEAF GRID

Multiples of 24/Tension 8-9
100% Chenille

Knit jacquard as in graph. Interesting effects can be achieved by using a mixture of yarns, colours and textures. Try using a really fine sewing thread with a standard 4-ply yarn. Try using rayon with lambswool and then felting the fabric. The wool will felt but the rayon will not, giving a bubbly effect. By running a fine lycra or elastic yarn with one of the yarns, a rich puckered effect is produced which can enhance this design.

TUCKS, LACE AND JACQUARD

Multiples of 24/Tension 6 and 8
Chenille and gold lurex cord

*K 2 rows col A (rust) T8.
Set for Fair Isle, col A in feeder A; col B (yellow) in feeder B.
K 1 repeat of PC. Change carriage to normal knitting.
K 2 rows col A.
Change to col C (gold cord) T6, K 6 rows. Pick up loops of last row of chenille and replace them on needles in work.
K 8 rows col C and using chenille loops again hook these onto needles in work. Alternate loops will serve to form the ridged pleats. Change to col D (white chenille) T8, K 1 row.
Transfer every 10th st onto the adjacent needle and push all empty needles into NWP. K 5 rows. Transfer the middle 5th st in every block onto its adjacent needle.
K 2 rows.

Transfer the 4th and 6th sts in every block onto their adjacent needles. Transfer st on L to L, st on R to R in each block.
K 2 rows.
Transfer the middle 5th st in every block onto adjacent needle and K 5 rows.
Change to col C, T6. K 8 rows and pick up loops of last row of chenille to form ridged pleat as before. K 6 rows and make ridged pleat remembering to use the loops of the chenille sts. This is important as the sts knitted in gold cord are tight and more difficult to manipulate. Repeat from *. On the jacquard sections reverse the colours of alternate repeats.

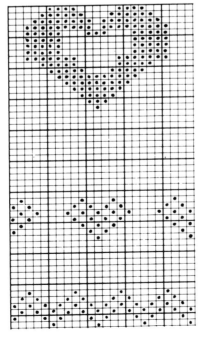

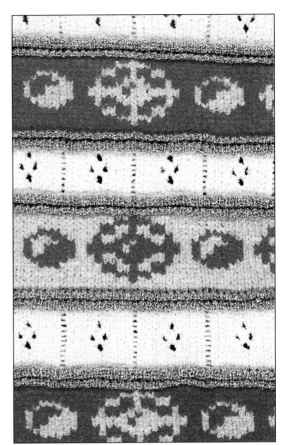

TUCKS, LACE AND JACQUARD

QUEEN OF HEARTS

Multiples of 24/Tension 7
Lambswool and fine rayon twist yarn

*K 14 rows col A (white).
Set carriage for weaving and insert PC.
K 6 rows col A feeder A, col B (green) in weaving yarn guide.
K 8 rows col A only.
K 7 rows col A feeder A; col C (rust) in weaving yarn guide.
K 14 rows col A only.
Set carriage to Fair Isle, col A feeder A; col D (rayon twist) feeder B.
K 17 rows then remove col D from feeder B. Set carriage for normal knitting.
Repeat from *.

To knit tube (piping) cast on 3 sts and knit a length in col A. Use this to decorate fabric by sewing on either as illustrated or to your own design. Chain stitch has also been used to embroider along the

small zig zag. The illustration shows sample before decoration and after.

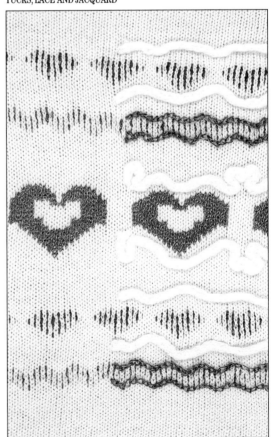

QUEEN OF HEARTS

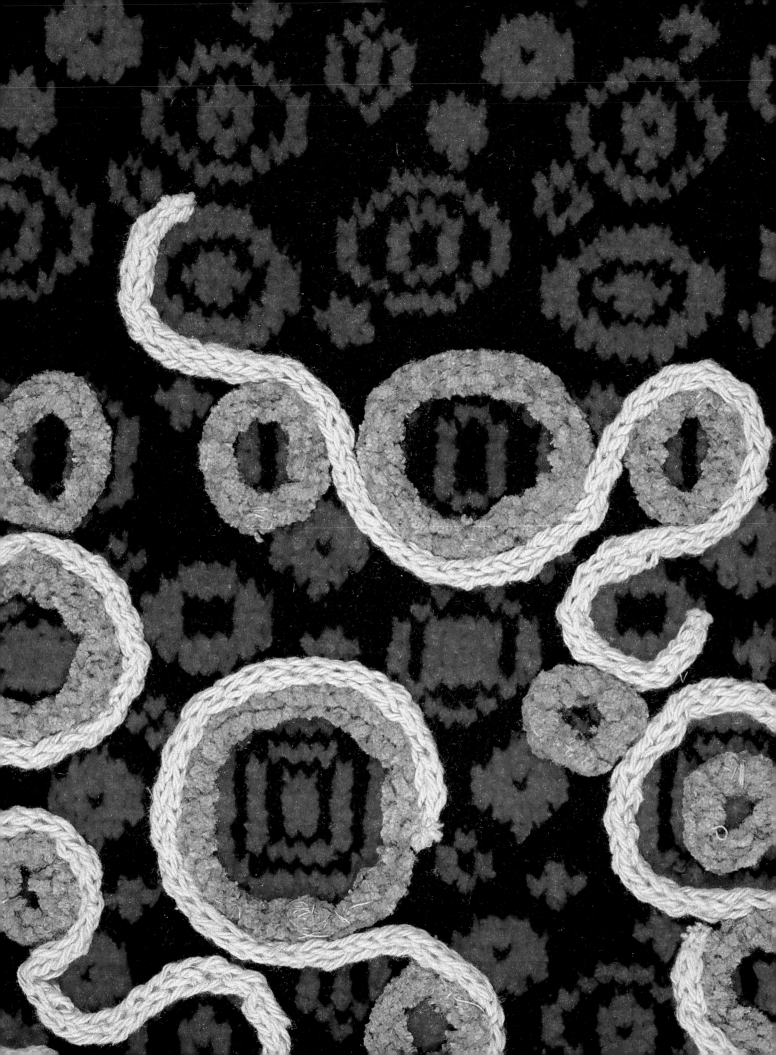

DAMASK

Multiples of 24/Tension 7
Acrylic and wool

As this design is knitted it shows a wide oval pattern. The distortion and linking of the shapes gives the design a rhythmic flowing appearance.

The top half of the illustration shows what happens to this design if you run one end of lycra or elastic yarn in with the main colour.

Colour sequence:
Col A (yellow) feeder A.
Col B (brown) feeder B.

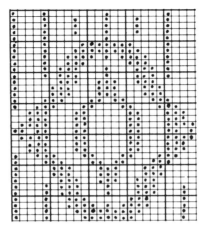

DAMASK

JACQUARD SNAKES

Multiples of 24/Tension 8
100% Chenille

Knit this design as in the graph with two colours then knit tubes to be sewn on to form snakes. These can be knitted in any yarn and any colour you find attractive. The ones illustrated are in green chenille and yellow cotton. To knit tubes, cast on 3 sts and knit a long length. This will automatically roll into a tube. Stitch these around a circle on the knitted jacquard then, using your second tube, form spirals round the circles. See illustration for guidance.

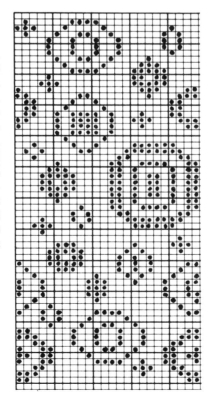

Left: JACQUARD SNAKES

TUCKED FLORAL BORDER

Multiples of 24 / Tension 7
100% Wool

Knit 12 rows col A (rust).
Set carriage to Fair Isle, col A in feeder A; col B (cream) in feeder B. K PC1 to row 46. Change to col C (purple) in feeder B. K 7 rows.
Set carriage for normal knitting and K 4 rows col A. Turn knitting round by using garter bar or by hand. Set carriage for tuck. Insert PC2 and K using 2 ends of yarn, one of col A and one of col C to complete swatch.
The turning of the knitting allows the reverse side of the tuck stitch to be used as the face side and so a very three-dimensional quality is produced together with the flat pattern of the jacquard.

TUCKED FLORAL BORDER

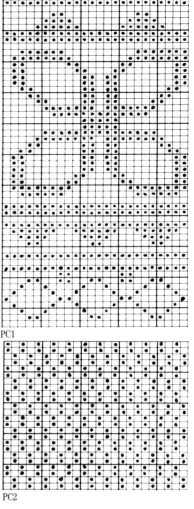

PC1

PC2

SMOCKED BOBBLE JACQUARD

Multiples of 12 / Tension 8
100% Cotton chenille

*K 4 rows col A (maroon). K 3 rows col B (navy). Pick up the loops of the sts from 1st row col B and hook onto needles in work. This forms a tucked pleat.
Repeat this sequence from * 3 more times (4 repeats).
K 5 rows col A. Switch to partial knitting and push 1st 5 needles into HP and next 4 into WP. Repeat this set out across the bed. K 6 rows col C (green). Return to normal knitting. K 5 rows col A.
K 3 rows col B and pick up loops of 1st row col B, hooking these onto the needles in work to form tucked pleat.
K 2 rows col A.

Switch to Fair Isle and set PC. With col B in feeder A and col A in feeder B, K one repeat of PC.
Return to normal knitting and K 2 rows col A. K 3 rows col B and pick up loops of 1st row col B to form tucked pleat.
Repeat pattern between ** and **. This is the repeat as illustrated. Finish off sample by chain stitch embroidery round partial knitting. See illustration for guidance.

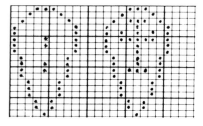

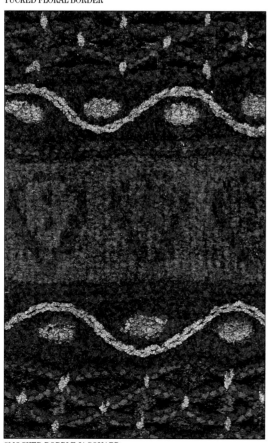

SMOCKED BOBBLE JACQUARD

CIRCLES

Multiples of 24/Tension 8
100% Chenille

This is a very simple jacquard which looks rich when knitted in textured yarns or a matt yarn with a shiny yarn.

Swiss darning could also be used to great effect. This method of embroidery on knitting is explained at the front of the book with the abbreviations.

Col A (black) feeder A.
Col B (red) feeder B.

CIRCLES

PRINCE OF WALES

JACQUARD BORDER LEAVES

Multiples of 24/Tension 7
Botany wool with fine twist yarn

K 2 rows col A (cream). Transfer every 3rd st onto adjacent needle on L.
K 6 rows col A.
Change to col B (rust), K 2 rows. Transfer every 3rd st onto adjacent needle on L.
K 2 rows col B, K 2 rows col A.
Set carriage to Fair Isle and insert PC.
Col A feeder A; col C (green) feeder B.
K 15 rows. K 3 rows col A only.
K 17 rows col A feeder A; col B feeder B.
K 7 rows col A feeder A only.
K 13 rows col A feeder A; col C feeder B.
Set carriage for normal knitting.
K 3 rows col A.
K 2 rows col B, then transfer every 3rd st onto adjacent needle on L.
K 2 rows col B.
Change to col A. K until swatch is size you want.

This design makes a wonderful border and it can be finished by adding a fringe. To make fringe thread 3 ends of col A through holes made at the start of the pattern and knot. When the swatch is complete put in a standard coloured wash in an automatic washing machine using pure soap rather than detergent and this will felt the wool, giving the finish illustrated here.

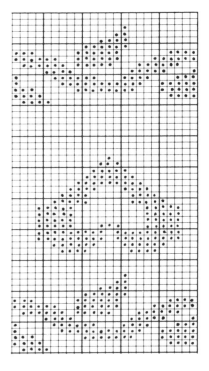

PRINCE OF WALES

Multiples of 4/Tension 7
100% cotton

Colour sequence:
MC (grey) constant feeder A.
The colour in feeder B is changed every 4 rows in the sequence yellow, lilac, red, sand, pink, green, rust, natural, blue.

This is the pattern used on the cover of this book. To achieve the Prince of Wales feathers effect, the fabric is used upside down. Although a very small repeat, this design can be made to look quite different by the use of colour; it looks effective worked in 2 colours only.

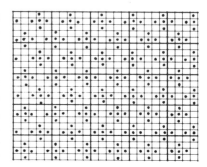

Right: JACQUARD BORDER LEAVES

92

SQUARES AND ZIG-ZAG

Multiples of 24/Tension 8

Version I

100% Shetland

This is quite a complex design and very effective in two colours.

Version II

100% Acrylic

The design was arranged to allow colour changes to be carried out that would give maximum effect to the pattern. An even richer design could be created by introducing more colours.

Colour sequence:
MC (green) constant in feeder A.
*2 rows col B (yellow) feeder B.
 5 rows col C (orange) feeder B.
 4 rows col B feeder B.
 5 rows col C feeder B.
 2 rows col B feeder B.
 4 rows col C feeder B.
 4 rows col B feeder B.
 4 rows col C feeder B.
 Repeat from *.

Version III

To create a soft Donegal look, Shetland (col C), wool tweed (MC) and wool multicolour (col B) are used.

Colour sequence:
MC constant feeder A.
 2 rows B feeder B.
 5 rows C feeder B.
 4 rows B feeder B.
 5 rows C feeder B.
 2 rows B feeder B.
 4 rows C feeder B.
 4 rows B feeder B.
 4 rows C feeder B.

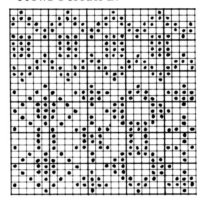

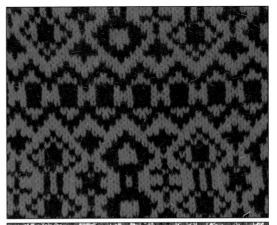

SQUARES AND ZIG-ZAG   Top: Version I   Above: Version III

DIAGONAL SQUARES

Multiples of 24/Tension 8
100% Acrylic

Version I

This is a classic design which looks quite dramatic when knitted in complementary colours. Not illustrated.

Version II

By changing the colour in feeder B every row it is possible to create a bird's-eye effect of some richness. It is important to start with each colour at the appropriate edge of the work as instructed in order to avoid cutting yarn and to allow for single row knitting.
Start with carriage on right.
Col A (green), C (blue) and E (pink) on right side of work.
Col B (rust) and D (orange) on left side of work.

Colour sequence:
MC (brown) constant feeder A.
1 row each col A, B, C, D, E in this sequence feeder B.
   The colour repeat does not match the pattern repeat which helps to give a random look.

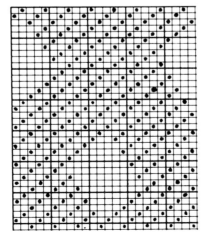

DIAGONAL SQUARES Version II

Left: SQUARES AND ZIG-ZAG Version II

ICELANDIC

ICELANDIC

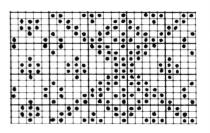

Multiples of 24/Tension 8
100% Shetland

This design was inspired by Icelandic designs and would lend itself to bright colours as well as the classic colours as illustrated.

Col A (white) feeder A.
Col B (navy) feeder B.

JACQUARD PLEATS

JACQUARD PLEATS

Multiples of 24/Tension 3 and 7
Fine and standard 3-ply cotton

*K 15 rows col A (fine cotton) T7.
 K 5 rows col B (brown).
 K 1 row col C (beige).
Set carriage for Fair Isle T3.
Insert PC 1. Col C feeder A; col B feeder B. K 8 rows. Set carriage to normal K. K 1 row col C.
K 5 rows col B. Pick up loops of first row col B before jacquard and hook onto the needles in work.
Repeat from *.

There are 3 different PC jacquard designs and these can be used in any sequence. The sequence illustrated is PC 1, 2, 3, 1, 3, 2, 1.

This design could be developed by the imaginative use of colour and different yarns. It could also be used on its side. Try your own interpretation.

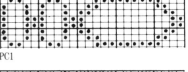

PC1

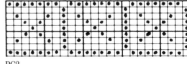

PC2

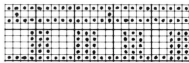

PC3

FRIGHTENED CATS

Multiples of 24/Tension 6
Acrylic and fine looped mohair

Set carriage for Fair Isle and insert PC.
*K 12 rows col A (purple).
K 8 rows col B (navy) with one end of fine elastic.
Col C (orange) feeder A; col D (blue) feeder B.
K 14 rows of PC.
K 8 rows col B with fine elastic feeder A, PC still running, no yarn feeder B.
K 29 rows of PC.
Col A feeder A; col E (green) feeder B.
K 8 rows col B with one end of elastic yarn, PC still running, no yarn feeder B.
K 20 rows col C feeder A; col D feeder B.
K 8 rows col B with one fine end of elastic feeder A, no yarn feeder B.
K 12 rows col A.
Repeat from *.

It is easier to leave the PC running throughout the pattern.

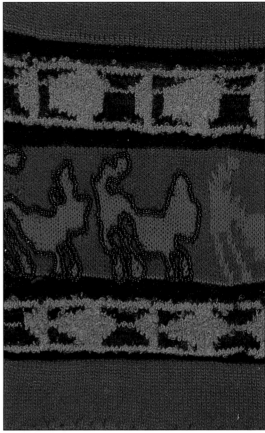

FRIGHTENED CATS

FLAGS

Multiples of 24/Tension 8
100% Shetland

Col A (green) feeder A.
Col B (black) feeder B.

If black remains constant and colour in feeder A changes every 12 rows, a wonderfully multi-coloured flag design can be produced.

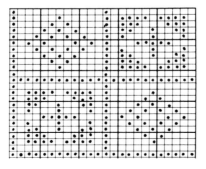

FLAGS

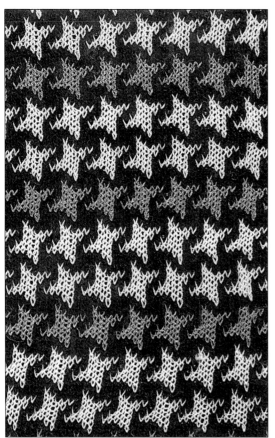

DOGTOOTH Version I

DOGTOOTH

This classic design is extremely useful and there are many ways to interpret it.

Version I

Tension 7
Black wool with rayon

MC (black wool) constant feeder A.

8 rows col A (cream rayon) feeder B.

8 rows col B (grey rayon) feeder B.

8 rows col C (white rayon) feeder B.

Version II

Tension 8
Black and white wool and Spancell

The Spancell shrink yarn is fed into the same feeder as the white wool. The black wool is fed in on its own. When finished the knitting is washed or steamed and the Spancell contracts pulling in the pattern as illustrated and giving an attractive three-dimensional look. The fabric is now elasticated and stretches. The qualities of the stretch fabric make it ideal for skirts. Lycra can be substituted for Spancell.

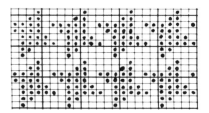

DOGTOOTH Version II

TURKISH DELIGHT

Multiples of 24/Tension 9
Snarl or towelling yarn with Shetland

This design looks rather ordinary if knitted simply in two colours but by adding a third colour which is also textured the design comes alive. It was inspired by old Kelim rugs from Turkey.

Colour sequence:

2 rows col A (green towelling) feeder A; col B (orange) feeder B.

11 rows col A feeder A; col C (black) feeder B.

8 rows col B feeder A; col C feeder B.

3 rows col A feeder A; col C feeder B.

8 rows col B feeder A; col C feeder B.

On the last row only the orange yarn knits and unfortunately to achieve the colour balance as illustrated the knitter is involved with odd row knitting. Different ways of feeding in the colour should be tried. A fourth colour might be striped in which would give a totally different colour balance to this pattern.

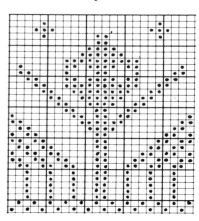

Right: TURKISH DELIGHT

CONES OF FLOWERS

Multiples of 24/Tension 6
100% Lambswool

K 50 rows col A (grey).
Transfer every other st to adjacent needle on L.
K 2 rows. Set carriage to Fair Isle and insert PC.
Col A feeder A; col B (white) feeder B.
Knit one repeat (66 rows).
Set carriage to normal knitting. K 22 rows col A. This completes the design.

This border can be used to edge garments, scarves or shawls. This jacquard can be enriched by Swiss darning over the pattern shapes as shown in the central cone. To add fringe take 3 ends of yarn thread these through the holes and knot. When knitting and decoration are complete, mill (felt) the sample. See notes on milling.

ABSTRACT GARDEN Version I

ABSTRACT GARDEN

This design is based on a flower garden by drawing the spaces between plants rather than the plants themselves. This way of producing a drawing automatically begins to look very abstract which can be exaggerated as it is here.

Version I
Multiples of 24/Tension 8
100% Acrylic

Col A (magenta) feeder A.
Col B (green) feeder B.

Version II
Multiples of 24/Tension 7
Shetland

MC (white) constant feeder A.
12 rows col B (purple) feeder B.
10 rows col C (dark blue) feeder B.

10 rows col D (light blue tweed) feeder B.
10 rows col E (mauve) feeder B.

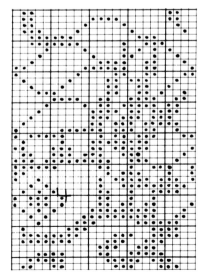

ABSTRACT GARDEN Version II

Left: CONES OF FLOWERS

ALPHABET TUCK

ALPHABET TUCK

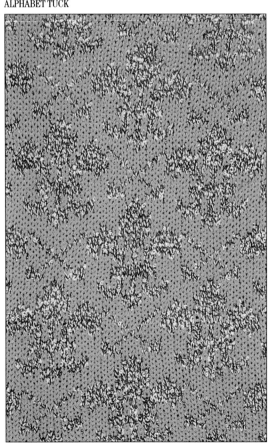

FLEUR-DE-LYS

Multiples of 24/Tension 4
Acrylic colours; gold lurex cord

*K 5 rows col A (yellow).
K 5 rows col B (gold). Pick up last 2 sts of every set of 8 in the 1st row of col A and replace these on needles in work.
K 5 rows col C (green).
K 5 rows col B. Pick up 1st row of col C as before.
Repeat this whole sequence from * once more.
K 10 rows col A.
K 10 rows col B.
K 5 rows col A.
K 5 rows col B. Pick up sts as before from 10 rows down.
K 5 rows col C.
K 5 rows col B. Pick up sts as before from 10 rows down.
K 5 rows col B.
K 5 rows col C.
Turn knitting by using a garter bar or by hand. Right side knitting now faces you.
K 10 rows col A. Pick up all sts from 1st row of col A and replace on needles in work. This creates a ridged pleat.
K 4 rows col C.
Set carriage for Fair Isle and insert PC1.
Col C in feeder A; col A in feeder B. Knit one complete repeat.
Reset carriage for normal knitting.
K 4 rows col C.
K 8 rows col A. Pick up all sts from 1st row col A and replace on needles as before to make ridged pleat.
K 10 rows col C. Pick up all sts from 1st row of col C and replace on needles as before to make ridged pleat.
K 12 rows col C.
Set carriage for Fair Isle. Insert PC2.
Col D (red) feeder A; col C feeder B.
Knit one complete repeat. Reset carriage for normal knitting.
K 5 rows col C.
K 6 rows col D. Pick up all sts from 1st row of col D as before to make ridged pleat.
K 3 rows col A. Turn knitting round using garter bar or by hand.
**K 5 rows col A.
K 5 rows col B. Pick up the last 2 sts in every set of 8 across your knitting and replace on corresponding needles. Repeat from ** for as many times as you wish.

This design could be adapted for many uses such as borders on sweaters or as an allover pattern. This is included in the book to stimulate invention regarding stitch combinations.

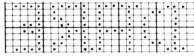

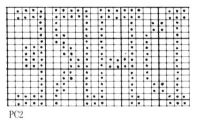

PC1

PC2

FLEUR-DE-LYS

Multiples of 24/Tension 8
Cotton and black-and-white wool tweed

This design if knitted with a mixture of textured and plain yarn can look extremely rich. Mohair could be used instead of the tweed yarn and then given a light brush which would add to the surface interest.

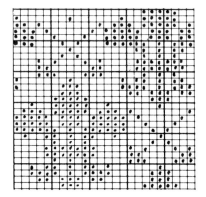

BROKEN BLOCKS

Multiples of 6
Chenille with fine embroidery yarn

This design relies on using a really fine yarn with a normal 4 ply. One illustration shows chenille with black-and-white very fine twisted embroidery thread. The tension is extremely important in achieving the right effect. It needs to be changed until you have the thick yarn knitting on as tight a tension as possible. Once you have decided on the tension, let the fine yarn take care of itself and knit; the effect can be extremely attractive. In experimenting try different yarn combinations. Two variations are illustrated.

Version I

Col A (yellow chenille) feeder A.
Col B (fine twist) feeder B.

Version II

Col B constant feeder A.
*2 rows col A feeder B.
  3 rows col C (green chenille)
    feeder B.
  3 rows col D (red chenille)
    feeder B.
  3 rows col E (violet chenille)
    feeder B.
  1 row col A feeder B.
  Repeat from *.

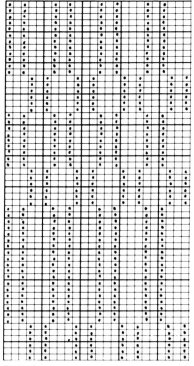

Version 1

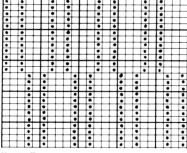

Version II

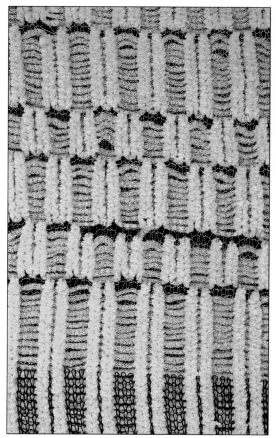

BROKEN BLOCKS Version I

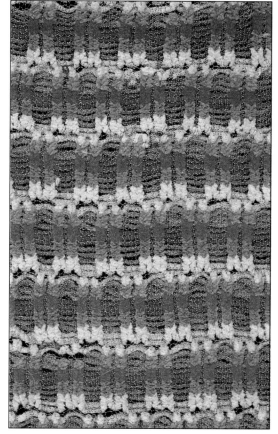

BROKEN BLOCKS Version II

CARNATION

Multiples of 24/Tension 8

Version I
Black wool and wool tweed

This design can be knitted with many different colour combinations and works well. Try using a fancy yarn for the flowers with a straight yarn background.

Version II
Blue acrylic, white cotton and Spancell.

This has a very fine end of shrink yarn (Spancell) run in with the white cotton. When the sample is steamed this shrink yarn contracts and becomes like elastic, hence the attractive puckering effect. Lycra can be substituted for Spancell.

Col A (blue acrylic) feeder A.
Col B (white cotton and Spancell) feeder B.

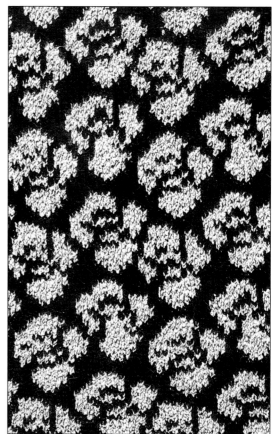

CARNATION Version I

BROKEN STRIPES

Multiples of 12/Tension 8

Version I
Tweed wool and brown Shetland

Set carriage for Fair Isle, insert PC. Start pattern. For Brother machines switch to KCII, otherwise the bird's-eye stitch may be distorted.

Version II
White rayon/mohair mixture and brown twisted Shetland.

Set machine as in Version I but transfer stitches from needles 8 and 10 onto needle 9 in every set of 12 across your knitting and push empty needles into NWP.

*6 rows col A (white) feeder A; col B (brown) feeder B.

6 rows col B feeder A; col A feeder B.
Repeat from *.

Try your own adaptations of this design.
On the graph, NWP is indicated by ⸾.

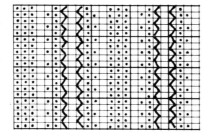

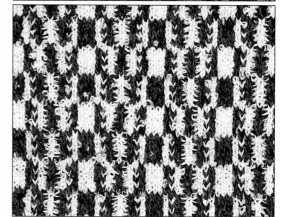

Left: CARNATION Version II

BROKEN STRIPES   Top: Version I   Above: Version II

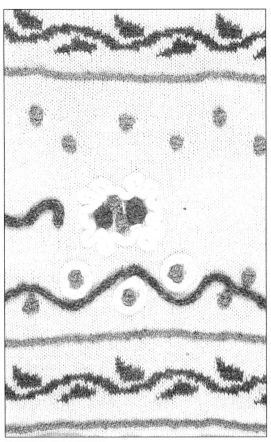

JACQUARD AND BOBBLES

BLOSSOM STRIPE

JACQUARD AND BOBBLES

Multiples of 24/Tension 5
Lambswool and fine rayon twist yarn

*K 8 rows col A (white).
K 6 rows col B (rust). Pick up sts of 1st row of col B and replace on needles in work. This forms ridged pleat.
K 8 rows col A.
Set carriage for Fair Isle, insert PC and K 1 repeat.
Col A feeder A, col C (green) feeder B.
Set carriage for normal knitting.
K 8 rows col A.
K 6 rows col B. Pick up sts from 1st row of col B and form ridged pleat as before.
K 12 rows col A.
Make bobbles: push all needles except 3 where bobble is to be knitted into HP (in this case needles 19, 20, 21 to L of Ø). Change to col B *.
K 6 rows then pick up sts from first row and replace on needles in work. Repeat this sequence twice.
Push these 3 needles into HP and push next 3 to be knitted into WP (needles 1, 1, 2); repeat from * to make bobbles. Repeat this sequence on needles 19, 20, 21 to R of Ø.
Set carriage for normal knitting and K 6 rows col A. Change to col B and make bobbles as before but on needles in position 29, 30, 31 to L of Ø, then needles 10, 11, 12 to L of Ø, then needles 10, 11, 12 to R of Ø and needles 29, 30, 31 to R of Ø, remembering to switch carriage to partial knitting.
Set carriage for normal knitting change to col A and K 20 rows. **
Change to col B, set carriage to partial knitting and make bobbles as before on needles 1, 2, 3 to R of Ø. Set carriage for normal knitting, K 1 row col A and change to partial knitting. Make bobble in col B on needles 4, 5, 6 to L of Ø and then on 4, 5, 6 to R of Ø. Set for normal knitting, K 1 row col A. Set carriage for partial knitting and make bobble in col B on needles 1, 2, 3 to L of Ø. Set carriage for normal knitting and using col A knit pattern in reverse from ** to start.

Decorate with piping. To make tube cast on 3 sts and knit. Sew this round bobbles and in and out of bobbles as illustrated or try your own decoration.

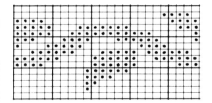

BLOSSOM STRIPE

Multiples of 24/Tension 8
Acrylic and cotton gimp yarn

Col A (black acrylic) feeder A.
Col B (white cotton gimp) feeder B.

By using cotton gimp yarn with a straight acrylic a lovely textured surface is created. The two yarns complement each other and add interest to the two-colour design. This stitch would also be attractive if multicolour yarn or space-dyed yarn was used in place of the cream cotton.

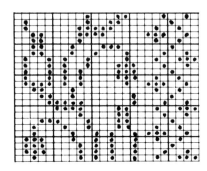

MULTI-JACQUARD

Multiples of 24/Tension 3
100% Acrylic

*K 11 rows col A (navy).
Set carriage for Fair Isle, insert PC and K with col A in feeder A and col B (purple) in feeder B.
K 6 rows col A in feeder A only.
K 4 rows col C (orange) in feeder A only.
K 4 rows col D (green) in feeder A only.
PC selecting needles again, K 27 rows col D in feeder A and col A in feeder B.
K 2 rows col D in feeder A only.
K 17 rows col D in feeder A and col C in feeder B.
K 2 rows col D in feeder A only.
K 4 rows col C in feeder A only.
Repeat from *.

Swiss darning has been used to enrich the design. See notes for this technique and illustration for guidance. It is much better if you work out your own Swiss darning pattern over the jacquard so that it is individual and unique.

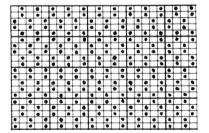

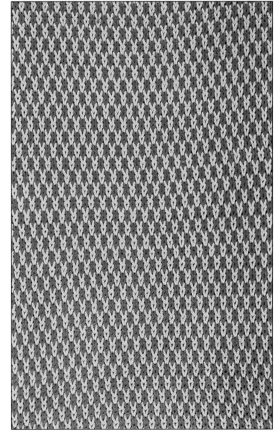

MULTI-JACQUARD

BIRD'S-EYE

Multiples of 2/Tension 8
100% Cotton

This very simple design can be extremely useful to mix with other patterns in one garment. The design lends itself to experimentation with colour striped into it. Mohair and rayon used together and then brushed give a wonderful soft textured effect.

BIRD'S-EYE

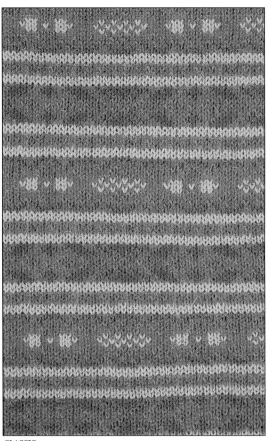

CLASSIC

CLASSIC

Multiples of 24/Tension 8
100% Shetland

This classic design knitted in two colours is quite effective but by using 4 colours and being prepared to change colours often and on odd rows this exciting kaleidoscope of pattern and colour can be produced.

Colour sequence:

2 rows col A (red) feeder A; col C (green) feeder B.

3 rows col A feeder A; col D (blue) feeder B.

3 rows col A feeder A; col B (yellow) feeder B.

3 rows col A feeder A; col D feeder B.

2 rows col A feeder A; col C feeder B.

2 rows col B feeder A; no yarn feeder B.

3 rows col A feeder A; col D feeder B.

2 rows col B feeder A; no yarn feeder B.

3 rows col A feeder A; col C feeder B.

3 rows col A feeder A; col D feeder B.

3 rows col A feeder A; col C feeder B.

2 rows col B feeder A; no yarn feeder B.

3 rows col A feeder A; col D feeder B.

2 rows col B feeder A; no yarn feeder B.

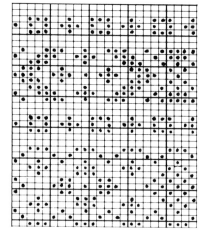

DAISY

Multiples of 24/Tension 8

Two versions of the daisy design are illustrated to show how very different it can look by using textured or multicoloured yarns. Experiment with changing the colour in feeder B on rows 15 and 30 which would give a striped multicolour floral design (Version III, not illustrated).

Version I

Col A (rust wool) feeder A.
Col B (turquoise rayon loop) feeder B.

Version II

Col A (black wool) feeder A.
Col B (multicolour acrylic) feeder B.

Version III

*15 rows col A feeder A; col B feeder B.

15 rows col A feeder A; col C feeder B.

15 rows col A feeder A; col D feeder B.

Repeat from *.

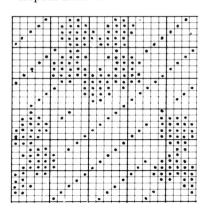

DAISY Version I

Right: DAISY Version II

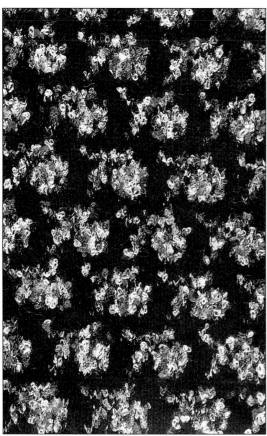

CHERRIES Version II

CHERRIES

Multiples of 12/Tension 8

Version I

100% Cotton perle

Col A (beige) feeder A.
Col B (plum) feeder B.
Not illustrated.

Version II

Black acrylic and rayon loop multicolour

If you wish to give this design an added three-dimensional quality brush the surface with a teasel brush. This breaks the rayon loops and produces a fluffy pile.

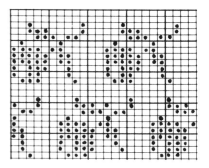

JACQUARD LETTERS

Multiples of 24/Tension 4
Acrylic colours; gold lurex cord

*K 4 rows col A (green).
Set carriage to Fair Isle and insert PC1 of letter R.
Knit one repeat using col A feeder A; col B (yellow) feeder B.
Reset carriage for normal knitting. K 10 rows col A.
K 9 rows col C (red) then transfer every alternate st to the adjacent needle.
K 9 rows. Pick up sts from first row of col C and replace on needles in work. This forms a picot hem.
Change to col D (gold). K 4 rows. Set carriage to Fair Isle and insert PC2.
Col A feeder A, col C feeder B, knit one repeat.
Reset carriage for normal knitting. K 1 row col C.
K 7 rows col D.
Pick up pairs of sts from 1st row of col D and replace them on needles about 8/12 sts apart.
K 2 rows col A. Set carriage for partial knitting. Push first 8 needles into HP. Leave next 3 in WP, next 6 into HP, next 3 into WP, next 4 needles into HP, next 3 into WP, next 7 into HP, next 3 into WP. Repeat across sample from L to R. K 6 rows col B and reset carriage for normal knitting.
K 6 rows col A.

K 1 row col D. Transfer every alternate st to its adjacent needle.
K 1 row col D. Transfer every 4th st to its adjacent needle.
K 2 rows col D. Repeat from *.

Many permutations are possible by moving the sequence of jacquard and the other elements of the design. Reorganise them and create a unique design from the swatch.

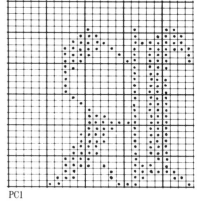

PC1

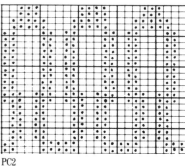

PC2

Right: JACQUARD LETTERS

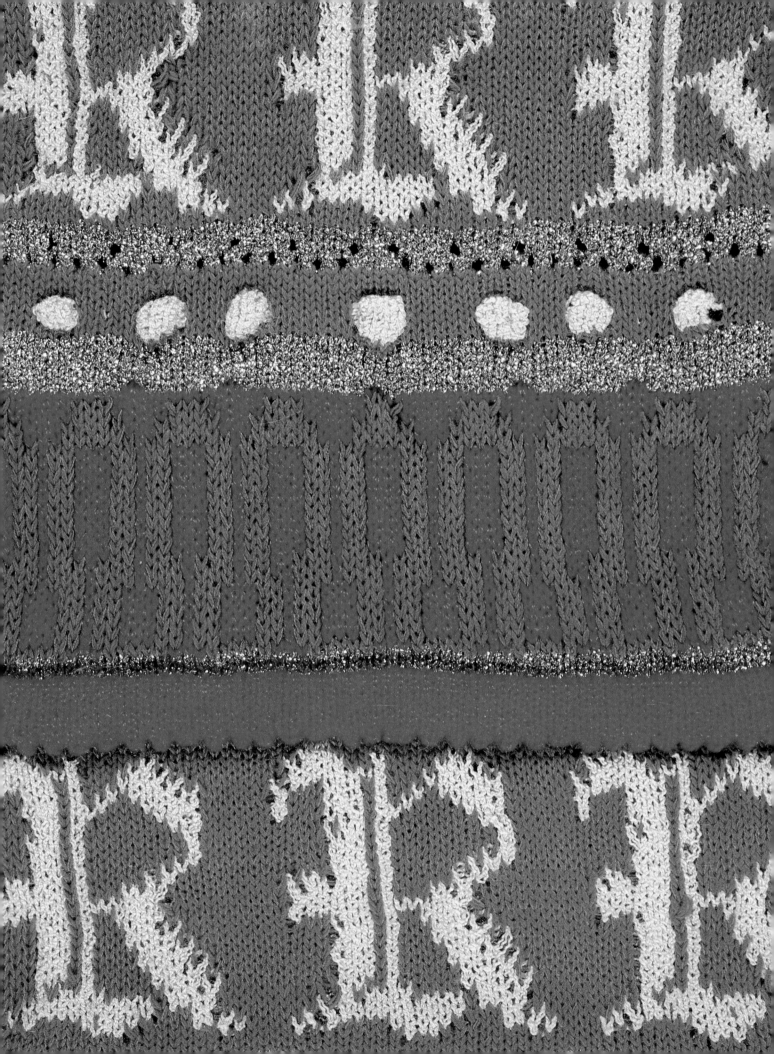

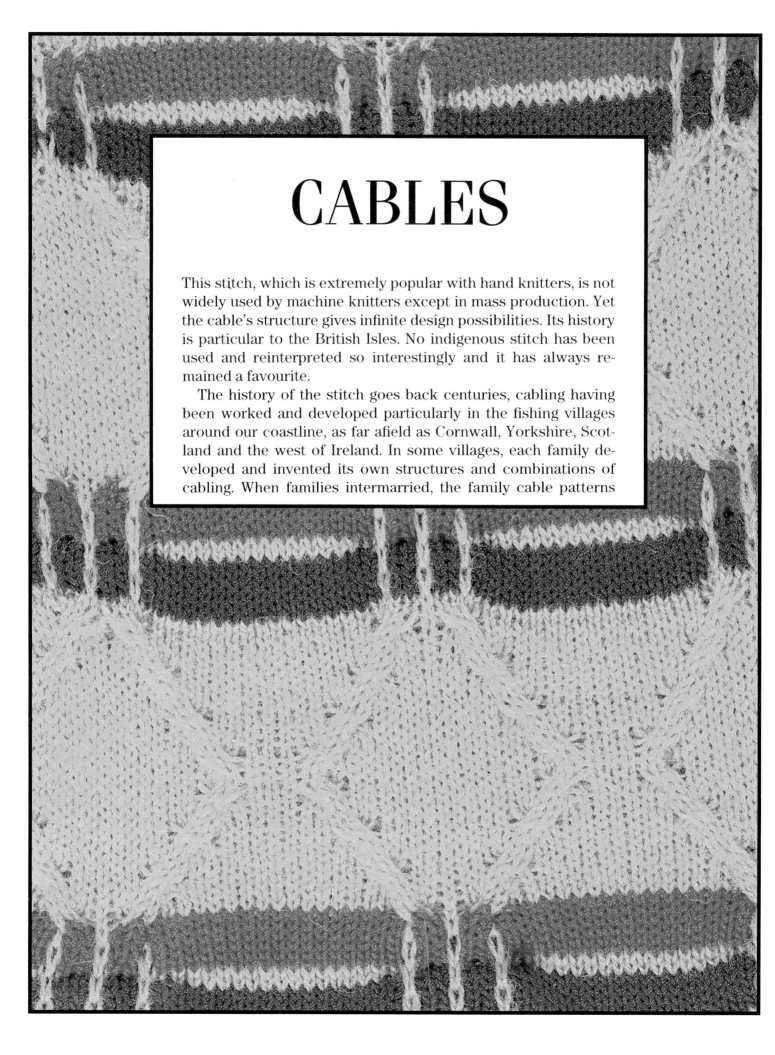

CABLES

This stitch, which is extremely popular with hand knitters, is not widely used by machine knitters except in mass production. Yet the cable's structure gives infinite design possibilities. Its history is particular to the British Isles. No indigenous stitch has been used and reinterpreted so interestingly and it has always remained a favourite.

The history of the stitch goes back centuries, cabling having been worked and developed particularly in the fishing villages around our coastline, as far afield as Cornwall, Yorkshire, Scotland and the west of Ireland. In some villages, each family developed and invented its own structures and combinations of cabling. When families intermarried, the family cable patterns

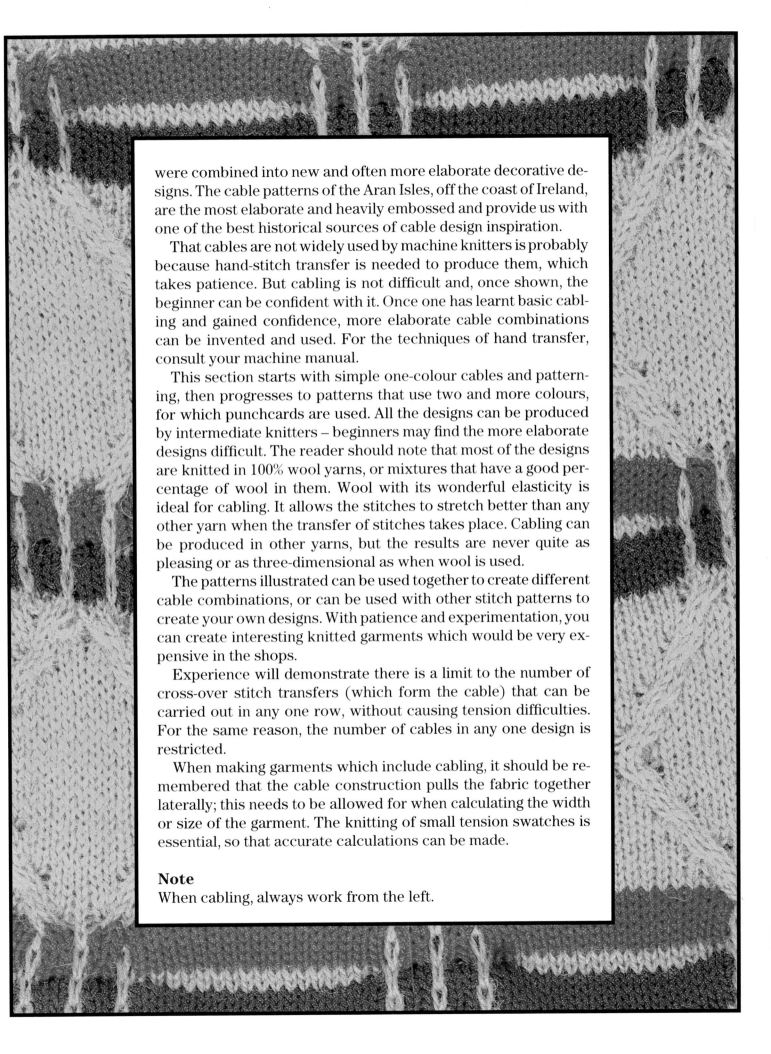

were combined into new and often more elaborate decorative designs. The cable patterns of the Aran Isles, off the coast of Ireland, are the most elaborate and heavily embossed and provide us with one of the best historical sources of cable design inspiration.

That cables are not widely used by machine knitters is probably because hand-stitch transfer is needed to produce them, which takes patience. But cabling is not difficult and, once shown, the beginner can be confident with it. Once one has learnt basic cabling and gained confidence, more elaborate cable combinations can be invented and used. For the techniques of hand transfer, consult your machine manual.

This section starts with simple one-colour cables and patterning, then progresses to patterns that use two and more colours, for which punchcards are used. All the designs can be produced by intermediate knitters – beginners may find the more elaborate designs difficult. The reader should note that most of the designs are knitted in 100% wool yarns, or mixtures that have a good percentage of wool in them. Wool with its wonderful elasticity is ideal for cabling. It allows the stitches to stretch better than any other yarn when the transfer of stitches takes place. Cabling can be produced in other yarns, but the results are never quite as pleasing or as three-dimensional as when wool is used.

The patterns illustrated can be used together to create different cable combinations, or can be used with other stitch patterns to create your own designs. With patience and experimentation, you can create interesting knitted garments which would be very expensive in the shops.

Experience will demonstrate there is a limit to the number of cross-over stitch transfers (which form the cable) that can be carried out in any one row, without causing tension difficulties. For the same reason, the number of cables in any one design is restricted.

When making garments which include cabling, it should be remembered that the cable construction pulls the fabric together laterally; this needs to be allowed for when calculating the width or size of the garment. The knitting of small tension swatches is essential, so that accurate calculations can be made.

Note
When cabling, always work from the left.

2 x 2 CABLE

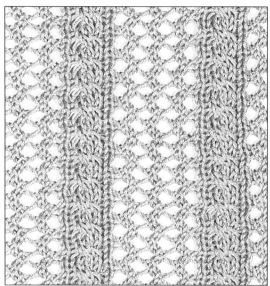

LACE AND CABLE STRIPE

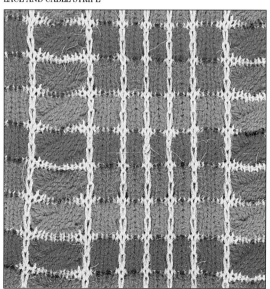

CABLED TUCK

2 x 2 CABLE

Multiples of 8/Tension 8
Shetland wool

Basic 2 x 2 cable repeats over 4 sts plus 4 sts between cables as illustrated. The spacing can be varied both vertically and horizontally. All the cables on this pattern are transferred L over R.

To work cable, pick up 2 right-hand sts of the 4 allowed for cable, then pick up the 2 left-hand sts. Transfer right-hand sts onto left-hand needles, and the left-hand sts onto the right-hand needles. This forms the cable. Repeat across the row with every alternate group of 4 needles.
K 4 rows and repeat.

This forms the cabling repeat as illustrated.

LACE AND CABLE STRIPE

Multiples of 12/Tension 7
100% Cotton

Although worked in just one colour, this pretty lace would look good in texture yarns and lurex. You can also experiment with colours to add interest.

Insert PC and set for lace.
Rows 1, 2, 3 and 4: K.
Row 5: *miss 7 sts, cable 4 sts, cross 2 sts at L over 2 sts at R, miss 1 st.
Repeat from *. K 1 row.
Repeat from row 1.

Note: the pattern is over 4 knitted rows, regardless of lace carriage movement.

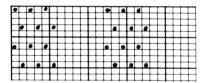

CABLED TUCK

Multiples of 24/Tension 8
100% Acrylic

PC punched in reverse.
Insert PC and set for tuck.
Rows 1, 2 and 3: K col A (yellow).
Rows 4, 5, 6 and 7: K col B (pink).
Row 8: *miss 2, cable 6 sts, crossing 3 at L over 3 at R, miss 16 sts. Repeat from *, K col B.
Rows 9 and 10: K col B.
Rows 11, 12 and 13: K col A.
Rows 14, 15, 16 and 17: K col C.
Row 18: *miss 2, cable 6 sts, crossing 3 at L over 3 at R, miss 16 sts. Repeat from *, K col C (green).

Rows 19 and 20: K col C.
Rows 21, 22 and 23: K col A.
Rows 24, 25, 26 and 27: K col D (blue).
Row 28: *miss 2 sts, cable 6 sts, crossing 3 sts at L over 3 sts at R, miss 16 sts.
Repeat from *, K 1 row.
Rows 29 and 30: K col D.

This sequence forms the total repeat.

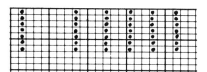

BIRD'S-EYE CABLE

Multiples of 12/Tension 8
4-ply 100% wool

The multiples of 12 needles become 10 when needles have been pushed into NWP, indicated on graph by ʅ.

Insert PC and set for Fair Isle, K 1 repeat. Transfer sts from needles 8 and 11 onto needles 9 and 12, in every repeat of 12 needles. Push empty needles out of action. Repeat this across the knitting. This makes the pattern repeat over 10 stitches with 2 needles out of work.
MC (yellow) feeder A; col B (lilac) feeder B.

Pattern
Rows 1, 2, 3 and 4: K.
Row 5: *miss 2 sts, cable 4 sts by crossing 2 sts from L over 2 sts at R, miss 4 sts. Repeat from *, K 1 row.
Rows 6, 7 and 8: K.
Row 9: *cable 4 sts by crossing 2 sts from L over 2 sts at R, miss 6 sts. Repeat from *. Repeat from row 1.

Cabling is always carried out on solid coloured areas. For those people with Brother machines, set the carriage switch to KC II if you have any problems with bird's-eye patterning.

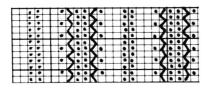

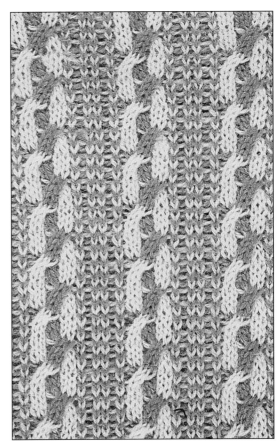
BIRD'S-EYE CABLE

CABLE SQUARES

Multiples of 36 sts/Tension 8
100% Wool

Cabled squares repeats over 18 sts plus 18 sts between squares. The 2nd repeat of the squares is moved to the position directly over the plain knitting and the plain knitting positioned above the last cabled square. These 2 repeats form the checker-board design. All cabling is done by transferring L sts over R sts.

Carriage on L.
Row 1: *miss 2 sts, cable 3, 4, 5 and 6 sts, miss 2 sts, cable 9, 10, 11 and 12 sts, miss 2 sts. Cable 15, 16, 17 and 18 sts, miss 18 sts. Repeat from *.
Rows 1, 2 and 3: K.
Row 4: K, *then cable 1, 2, 3 and 4 sts, miss 2 sts, cable 7, 8, 9 and 10 sts, miss 2 sts, cable 13, 14, 15 and 16 sts, miss 20 sts. Repeat from *.
Rows 5, 6 and 7: K.
Row 8: work as row 1.

Rows 9, 10 and 11: K.
Row 12: work as row 4.
Rows 13, 14 and 15: K.
Row 16: work as row 1.
Rows 17, 18 and 19: K.
Row 20: work as row 4.
Rows 21, 22 and 23: K.
Row 24: K, *miss 20 sts, cable 21, 22, 23 and 24 sts, miss 2 sts, cable 27, 28, 29 and 30 sts, miss 2 sts, cable 33, 34, 35 and 36 sts. Repeat from *.
Rows 25, 26 and 27: K.
Row 28: K, *miss 18 sts, cable 19, 20, 21 and 22 sts, miss 2 sts, cable 25, 26, 27 and 28 sts, miss 2 sts, cable 31, 32, 33 and 34 sts, miss 2 sts. Repeat from *.
Rows 29, 30 and 31: K.
Row 32: K cable as row 24.
Rows 33, 34 and 35: K.
Row 36: K and cable as row 28.
Rows 37, 38 and 39: K.
Row 40: K and cable as row 24.
Rows 41, 42, 43 and 44: K and repeat from row 1.

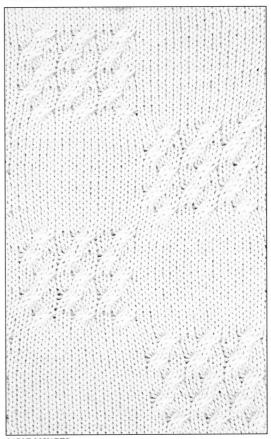
CABLE SQUARES

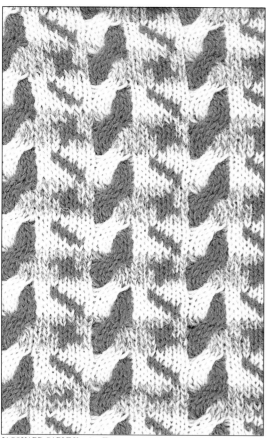

JACQUARD CABLE Version II

JACQUARD CABLE

Multiples of 12/Tension 8

This is a cable stitch combined with a simple jacquard to form a patterned stripe between the cabling.

Insert PC and set for Fair Isle.
Row 1: *miss 1 st, cable 6 sts, crossing 3 sts at L over 3 sts at R, miss 5 sts. Repeat from *, K 1 row.
Rows 2, 3, 4, 5 and 6: K.
Row 7: work as row 1.
Rows 8, 9, 10, 11 and 12: K.
This forms the repeat.

Version I
100% Wool
6 rows col A (blue) feeder B; col B (red) feeder A.
6 rows feeder C (green) feeder B; col B feeder A.

6 rows col D (yellow) feeder B; col B feeder A.

Version II
Tweed and wool
6 rows col A (blue wool) feeder B; col B (white wool) feeder A.
6 rows col A feeder B; col C (grey tweed) feeder A.

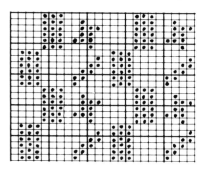

SQUARES AND CABLE CHECK

Multiples of 16/Tension 8
100% Wool

Rows 1-7: K.
Row 8: *cable 4 sts, crossing 2 sts at R over 2 sts at L, miss 12 sts. Repeat from *, K 1 row.
Rows, 9, 10 and 11: K.
Row 12: *miss 5 sts, cable 4 sts, crossing 2 sts at L over 2 sts at R, miss 2 sts, cable 4 sts, crossing 2 sts at L over 2 sts at R, miss 1 st. Repeat from *, K 1 row.
Rows 13, 14 and 15: K.
Row 16: cable 4 sts, crossing 2 sts at L over 2 sts at R, miss 12 sts. Repeat from *, K 1 row.
Rows 17, 18, 19, 20, 21, 22 and 23: K.
Row 24: *cable 4 sts, crossing 2 sts at R over 2 sts at L, miss 12 sts. Repeat from *, K 1 row.

Rows 25, 26, 27, 28, 29, 30 and 31: K.
Row 32: work as row 16.
Rows 33, 34 and 35: K.
Row 36: work as row 12.
Rows 37, 38 and 39: K.
Row 40: work as row 24.
Rows 41, 42, 43, 44, 45, 46 and 47: K.
Row 48: work as row 16.
This forms the total repeat of 48 rows from row 1.
This pattern makes the square and cable design.

To enhance this, fabric crayons have been used together with decoration to add more pattern and colour interest.

You could also try your own fabric crayon design on the cable squares and use your own colour combinations.

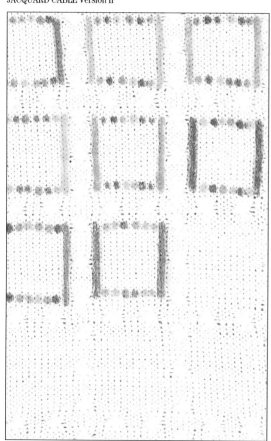

SQUARES AND CABLE CHECK

Right: JACQUARD CABLE Version I

TWO-COLOURED CABLE

Multiples of 12/Tension 8
4-ply 100% Wool

Set for Fair Isle and insert PC.
Col A (navy) feeder A.
Col B (rust) feeder B.
K 6 rows, cable 3 sts col B with 3 sts col A.
K 6 rows, cable 3 sts col B with 3 sts col A.

This sequence is the repeat.

Always cable R sts onto L needles, then L sts onto R needles.

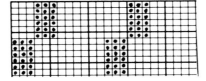

BOY'S OWN

Multiples of 24/Tension 8
Wool and cotton

PC punched in reverse.
Insert PC and set for tuck. When cabling, start from left.
**Rows 1, 2, 3, 4, 5 and 6: K col A (red).
Rows 7 and 8: K col B (yellow).
Rows 9, 10, 11, 12, 13 and 14: K col C (blue).
Rows 15 and 16: K col B.
Row 17: *miss 7 sts, cable 4 sts, crossing 2 sts at L over 2 sts at R, miss 1 st, cable 4 sts, crossing 2 sts at R over 2 sts at L, miss 8 sts. Repeat from *, K 1 row.
Rows 18, 19 and 20: K.
Row 21: *miss 5 sts, cable 4 sts, crossing 2 sts at L over 2 sts at R, miss 5 sts, cable 4 sts, crossing 2 sts at R over 2 sts at L, miss 6 sts. Repeat from *, K 1 row.
Rows 22, 23 and 24: K.
Row 25: *miss 3 sts, cable 4 sts, crossing 2 sts at L over 2 sts at R, miss 9 sts, cable 4 sts, crossing 2 sts at R over 2 sts at L, miss 4 sts. Repeat from *, K 1 row.
Rows 26, 27 and 28: K.
Row 29: *miss 1 st, cable 4 sts, crossing 2 sts at L over 2 sts at R, miss 13 sts, cable 4 sts, crossing 2 sts at R over 2 sts at L, miss 2 sts. Repeat from *, K 1 row.
Rows 30, 31 and 32: K.
Row 33: *miss 1 st, cable 4 sts, crossing 2 sts at R over 2 sts at L, miss 13 sts, cable 4 sts, crossing 2 sts at L over 2 sts at R, miss 2 sts. Repeat from *, K 1 row.
Rows 34, 35 and 36: K.
Row 37: *miss 3 sts, cable 4 sts, crossing 2 sts at R over 2 sts at L, miss 9 sts, cable 4 sts, crossing 2 sts at L over 2 sts at R, miss 4 sts. Repeat from *, K 1 row.
Rows 38, 39 and 40: K.
Row 41: *miss 5 sts, cable 4 sts, crossing 2 sts at R over 2 sts at L, miss 5 sts, cable 4 sts, crossing 2 sts at R over 2 sts at L, miss 6 sts. Repeat from *, K 1 row.
Rows 42, 43 and 44: K.
Row 45: *miss 7 sts, cable 4 sts, crossing 2 sts at R over 2 sts at L, miss 1 st, cable 4 sts, crossing 2 sts at L over 2 sts at R, miss 8 sts. Repeat from *, K 1 row.
Row 46: K.
Repeat from **.

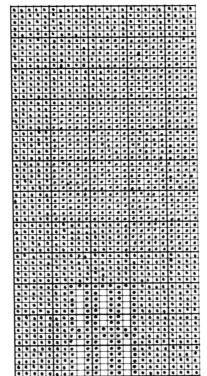

Left: BOY'S OWN

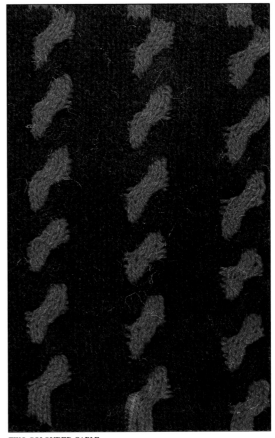

TWO-COLOURED CABLE

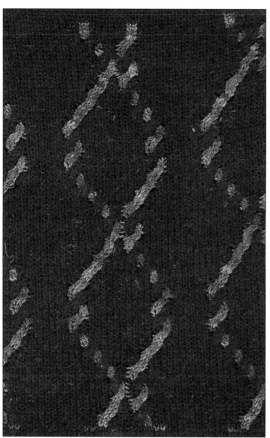

DIAMOND FENCE CABLE

DIAMOND FENCE CABLE

Multiples of 24/Tension 8
Shetland wool

Insert PC and set for Fair Isle.
Row 1: * in each set of 24, miss 9
sts, cable 4 sts by crossing 2 left-
hand sts over 2 right-hand sts,
cable 4 sts by crossing 2 left-hand
sts over 2 right-hand sts, miss 7
sts. Repeat from *, K 1 row.
Rows 2, 3 and 4: K.
Row 5: work as row 1.
Rows 6, 7 and 8: K.
Row 9: *miss 7 sts, cable 4 sts by
transferring 2 left-hand sts over 2
right-hand sts, miss 2 sts, cable 4
sts crossing 2 left-hand sts over 2
right-hand sts, miss 7 sts. Repeat
from *, K 1 row.
Rows 10, 11 and 12: K.
Row 13: *miss 5 sts, cable 4 sts,
crossing 2 left-hand sts over 2
right-hand sts, miss 6 sts, cable 4
sts, crossing 2 left-hand sts over 2
right-hand sts, miss 5 sts. Repeat
from *, K 1 row.
Rows 14, 15 and 16: K.
Row 17: *miss 3 sts, cable 4 sts,
crossing 2 left-hand sts over 2
right-hand sts, miss 10 sts, cable 4
sts, cross 2 left-hand sts over 2
right-hand sts, miss 3 sts. Repeat
from *, K 1 row.
Rows 18, 19 and 20: K.
Row 21: work as row 17.
Rows 22, 23 and 24: K.
Row 25: work as row 17.
Rows 26, 27 and 28: K.

Row 29: work as row 17.
Rows 30, 31 and 32: K.
Row 33: *miss 5 sts, cable 4 sts by
crossing 2 left-hand sts over 2
right-hand sts, miss 6 sts, cable 4
sts, cross 2 left-hand sts over 2
right-hand sts, miss 5 sts. Repeat
from *, K 1 row.
Rows 34, 35 and 36: K.
Row 37: *miss 7 sts, cable 4 sts,
crossing 2 left-hand sts over 2
right-hand sts, miss 2 sts, cable 4
sts, cross 2 left-hand sts over 2
right-hand sts, miss 7 sts. Repeat
from *, K 1 row.
Rows 38, 39 and 40: K.
Return to row 1. This forms the
repeat.

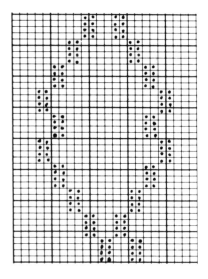

ARAN

Multiples of 24/Tension 8
Acrylic main colour and rayon tweed yarn
Two-coloured jacquard with cabling

Insert PC and set for Fair Isle.
Row 1: * in each set of 24 sts, miss 4 sts, cable 4 sts crossing 2 sts at R over 2 sts at L, miss 2 sts, cable 4 sts crossing 2 sts at L over 2 sts at R, miss 2 sts, cable 4 sts crossing 2 sts at L over 2 sts at R, miss 4 sts. Repeat from *. K 1 row.
Rows 2, 3 and 4: K.
Row 5: *miss 4 sts, cable 4 sts crossing 2 sts at L over 2 sts at R, miss 2 sts, cable 4 sts crossing 2 sts at L over 2 sts at R, miss 2 sts, cable 4 sts crossing 2 sts at R over 2 sts at L, miss 4 sts. Repeat from *. K 1 row.
Rows 6, 7 and 8: K.
Row 9: *miss 6 sts, cable 4 sts crossing 2 sts at L over 2 sts at R, cable 4 sts crossing 2 sts at L over 2 sts at R, cable 4 sts crossing 2 sts at R over 2 sts at L, miss 6 sts. Repeat from *. K 1 row.
Rows: 10, 11 and 12: K.
Row 13: *miss 8 sts, cable 4 sts crossing 2 sts at L over 2 sts at R, cable 4 sts crossing 2 sts at R over 2 sts at L, miss 8 sts. Repeat from *. K 1 row.

Rows 14, 15 and 16: K.
Row 17: *miss 10 sts, cable 4 sts crossing 2 sts at R over 2 sts at L, miss 10 sts. Repeat from *. K 1 row.
Rows 18, 19 and 20: K.
Row 21: *miss 8 sts, cable 4 sts crossing 2 sts at R over 2 sts at L, cable 4 sts crossing 2 sts at L over 2 sts at R, miss 8 sts. Repeat from *. K 1 row.
Rows 22, 23 and 24: K.
Row 25: *miss 6 sts, cable 4 sts crossing 2 sts at R over 2 sts at L, cable 4 sts crossing 2 sts at L over 2 sts at R, cable 4 sts crossing 2 sts at L over 2 sts at R, miss 6 sts. Repeat from *. K 1 row.
Rows 26, 27 and 28: K.
Repeat from start.

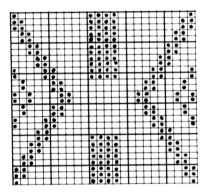

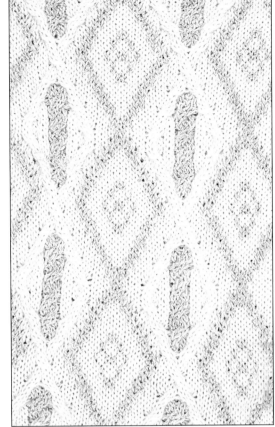

ARAN

CABLE CLASSIC

Multiples of 12/Tension 8
4-ply 100% Wool

Rows 1, 2, 3, 4, 5 and 6: K.
Row 7: *miss 6 sts, cable 6 sts, crossing 3 sts at L over 3 sts on R, miss 6 sts, cable 6 sts, crossing 3 sts at L over 3 sts on R. Repeat from *.
Rows 8, 9, 10, 11, 12 and 13: K.
Row 14: work as row 7.
Repeat from row 1.

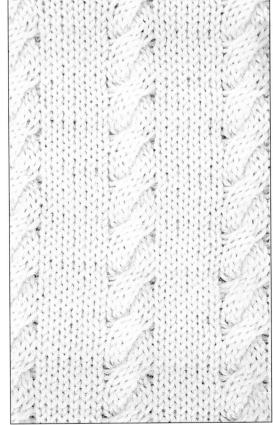

CABLE CLASSIC

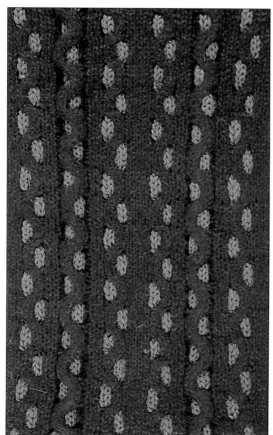

S AND Z CABLE Version I

CORDED CABLE

S AND Z CABLE

Multiples of 12/Tension 8
Acrylic gimp and wool

Needle set-out
·111111·1111·111111·1111

Version I
*K 10 rows. Using 2 three-pronged transfer tools, lift the sts from the 1st set of 6 needles and transfer the sts from L to R and R to L. Carry out this same sequence with the next set of 6 sts. This time transfer the sts from R to L and L to R. Repeat this across the knitting.

K 10 rows. Repeat the sequence above, but this time reverse the direction of transference. This creates the waving lines.
Repeat from *.

Version II
K as above.
When sample is large enough, knit a cord and thread it through the twists of the cable. Do not pull this too tight but allow it to flow with the curves of the cable.

The cord is knitted over 5 needles in the normal way and can be worked in any colour.

CORDED CABLE

Multiples of 24/Tension 8
Acrylic gimp and wool

Set for Fair Isle. Insert PC and col A (navy) feeder A; col B (green) feeder B.
K 12 rows, transfer sts on needles 15 and 22 of every repeat of 24 onto adjacent needles and push empty needles into NWP, marked { on graph. Repeat this across your knitting.
Transfer sts marked × on graph.
*K 6 rows.
On 1st row of the pattern change-over, cable 2 sts col A over 2 sts col B, miss 4 sts, cable 2 sts col A over 2 sts col B, miss 2 sts, cable 3 sts over 3 sts, both col A, miss 2 sts, repeat from * across your knitting, cabling R to L.
K 6 rows.

**On 1st row of the pattern change over, cable 2 sts col A over 2 sts col B, miss 4 sts, cable 2 sts col A over 2 sts col B, miss 2 sts, cable 3 sts over 3 sts col A, miss 2 sts. Repeat from ** across your knitting. Cabling L to R.
Repeat from *. This completes the pattern sequence.

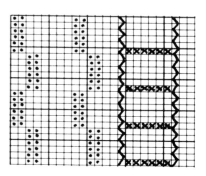

Right: S AND Z CABLE Version II

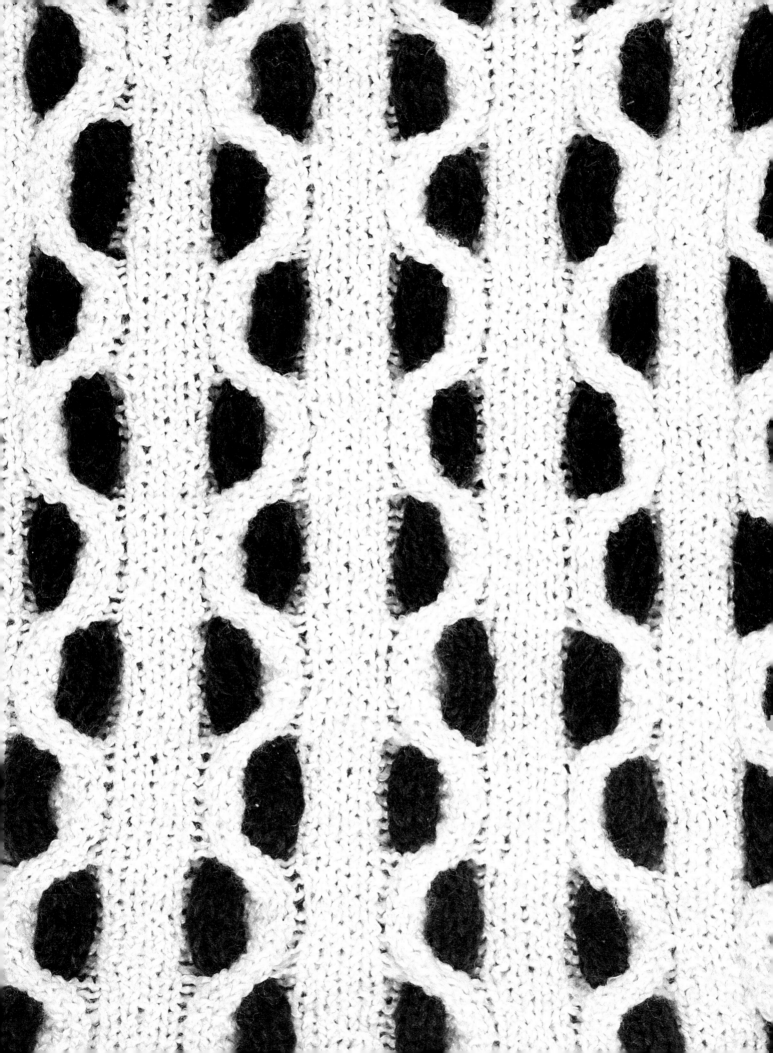

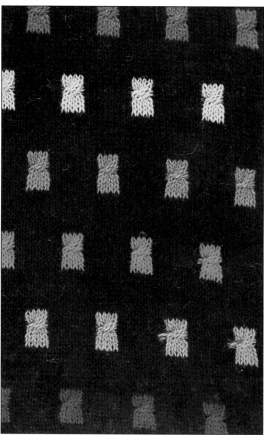

BROKEN CABLES

BROKEN CABLES

Multiples of 12/Tension 8
Shetland wool

This simple two-coloured jacquard has been enhanced by the introduction of cabling. Each time the jacquard pattern comes into work, a second colour is introduced. All the cables – ie, jacquard squares – could be just one colour.

After knitting rows 14 and 32, cable 4 sts of the pattern colour, crossing 2 right-hand sts first. This creates a cable that goes from L to R. It is possible to check that the cabling is being worked on the correct row as the stitch transfer always takes place on row 5 of the coloured square.

Colour sequences:
*9 rows MC (bottle green) feeder A throughout.
 9 rows col B (emerald) feeder B.
 9 rows feeder B empty.

9 rows col C (lilac) feeder B.
9 rows feeder B empty.
9 rows col D (red) feeder B.
9 rows feeder B empty.
9 rows col E (blue) feeder B.
9 rows feeder B empty.
9 rows col F (yellow) feeder B.
Repeat from *.

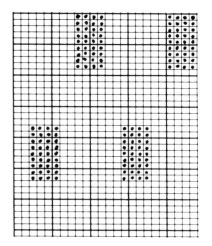

BRICK CABLE

Multiples of 14/Tension 8
100% Acrylic

In all cables, 2 sts are crossed from L over 2 sts at R.
Rows 1-4: K.
Row 5: *miss 10 sts, cable 4 sts as directed. Repeat from *, K 1 row.
Rows 6, 7 and 8: K.
Row 9: *miss 8 sts, cable 4 sts, miss 2 sts. Repeat from *, K 1 row.
Rows 10, 11 and 12: K.
Row 13: *miss 10 sts, cable 4 sts. Repeat from *, K 1 row.
Rows 14, 15 and 16: K.
Row 17: *miss 8 sts, cable 4 sts, miss 2 sts. Repeat from *, K 1 row.

Rows 18, 19 and 20: K.
Row 21: *miss 1 st, cable 4 sts, miss 9 sts. Repeat from *, K 1 row.
Rows 22, 23 and 24: K.
Row 25: *miss 3 sts, cable 4 sts, miss 7 sts. Repeat from *, K 1 row.
Rows 26, 27 and 28: K.
Row 29: *miss 1 st, cable 4 sts, miss 9 sts. Repeat from *, K 1 row.
Rows 30, 31 and 32: K.
Row 33: *miss 3 sts, cable 4 sts, miss 7 sts. Repeat from *, K 1 row.
Rows 34, 35 and 36: K.
Row 37: *miss 1 st, cable 4 sts, miss 9 sts. Repeat from *, K 1 row.
Rows 38, 39 and 40: K. Repeat from row 5.

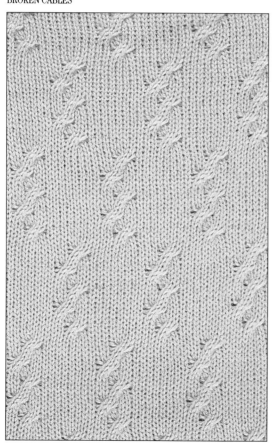

BRICK CABLE

DRAUGHT BOARD

Multiples of 24/Tension 8
100% Wool and Shetland tweed

Insert PC and set for Fair Isle.
Col A (white) feeder A.
Col B (tweed) feeder B.
*K PC until white pattern appears in tweed squares, then in each tweed square cable as follows:
Miss 2 sts, cable 2 sts col A over 2 sts col B, L to R twice, miss 2 sts, repeat across knitting.
K PC until pattern appears again in tweed squares (6 rows), then in each tweed square:
Miss 2 sts, cable 2 sts col B over 2 sts col A, L to R twice, miss 2 sts, repeat across knitting.
Repeat from *.
This sequence of cabling is repeated each time the pattern changes in the tweed squares. The position of the squares is also staggered on the PC to form a chequer board. Repeat the sequence up the knitting.

Always cable right-hand sts first, crossing R sts onto left-hand needles and then L sts onto right-hand needles, working within the blocks of Shetland twist.

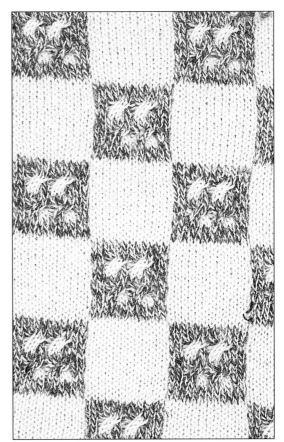

DRAUGHT BOARD

ZIG-ZAG CABLE

Multiples of 18/Tension 8
Shetland wool

Rows 1-6: K.
Row 7: *cable 1st 6 sts, crossing 3 sts at L over 3 sts at R, miss 2 sts, cable 4 sts, crossing 2 sts at R over 2 sts at L, miss 6 sts. Repeat from * across row, K 1 row.
Rows 8, 9 and 10: K.
Row 11: *miss 10 sts, cable 4 sts, crossing 2 sts at L over 2 sts at R, miss 4 sts. Repeat from * across row, K 1 row.
Row 12: K.
Row 13: *cable 1st 6 sts, crossing 3 sts at L over 3 sts at R, miss 12 sts. Repeat from *, K 1 row.
Row 14: K.
Row 15: *miss 12 sts, cable 4 sts, crossing 2 sts at L over 2 sts at R, miss 2 sts. Repeat from *, K 1 row.
Rows 16, 17 and 18: K.
Row 19: *cable 1st 6 sts, crossing 3 sts at L over 3 sts at R, miss 6 sts, cable 4 sts, crossing 2 sts at L over 2 sts at R, miss 2 sts. Repeat from *, K 1 row.
Rows 20, 21 and 22: K.
Row 23: *miss 10 sts, cable 4 sts, crossing 2 sts at R over 2 sts at L, miss 4 sts. Repeat from *, K 1 row.
Row 24: K.
Row 25: *cable 1st 6 sts, crossing 3 sts at L over 3 sts at R, miss 12 sts. Repeat from *, K 1 row.
Row 26: K.
Row 27: *miss 8 sts, cable 4 sts, crossing 2 sts at R over 2 sts at L, miss 6 sts. Repeat from *, K 1 row.
Rows 28, 29 and 30: K.

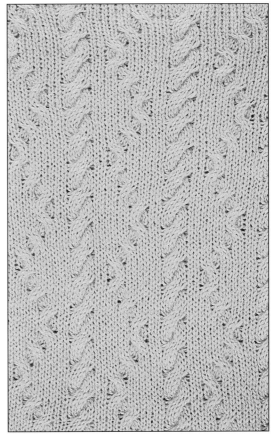

ZIG-ZAG CABLE

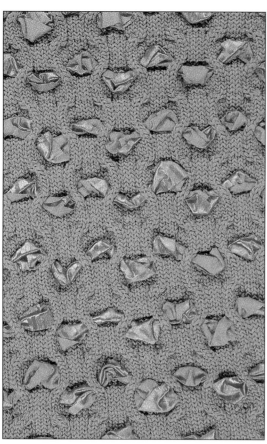

RIBBON CABLE

RIBBON CABLE

Multiples of 9/Tension 8
100% Wool with ribbon

Needle set-out 1111·111·1111·111·

*K 8 rows. Using 2 two-pronged transfer tools, lift the sts from the 1st set of 4 needles and cross them R to L and L to R to form a cable. With the 2nd set of 4 needles, transfer the sts in the opposite direction – ie, L to R and R to L. Repeat these 2 cables across the knitting.
K 8 rows. With 2 two-pronged transfer tools, lift the sts from the 1st set of 4 needles and transfer them L to R and R to L to form a cable. With the 2nd set of 4 nee-

dles, transfer the sts in the opposite direction. Repeat these 2 cables across the knitting. Repeat from *. When the swatch is large enough, cast off and thread the ribbon horizontally through the holes created by the cables. Do not pull this too tight but allow it to flow with the curves of the cable.

In the sample, a sateen fabric was cut into 1in (25mm) strips and threaded through the holes. A variety of colours could be used or different fabrics if a more decorative look were required. Printed fabric cut into strips could look very interesting.

UNRAVELLING DIAMONDS CABLE

Multiples of 24/Tension 8
100% Wool

Set for Fair Isle. Insert PC and MC (black) feeder A throughout.
Col A (blue) feeder B.
*Rows 1, 2, 3 and 4: K.
Miss 8 sts, cable 4 sts, crossing 2 sts at L over 2 sts at R. Miss 12 sts. Repeat across knitting.
Rows 5, 6, 7 and 8: K. Col B (red) in feeder B. Miss 6 sts, cable 4 sts, crossing 2 sts at L over 2 sts at R, miss 2 sts, cable 4 sts, crossing 2 sts at R over 2 sts at L, miss 8 sts. Repeat across knitting.
Rows 9, 10, 11 and 12: K. Col C (yellow) feeder B. Miss 4 sts, cable 4 sts, crossing 2 sts at L over 2 sts at R, miss 6 sts, cable 4 sts, crossing 2 sts at R over 2 sts at L, miss 6 sts. Repeat across knitting.
Rows 13, 14, 15 and 16: K. Col A feeder B. Miss 2 sts, cable 4 sts, crossing 2 sts at L over 2 sts at R, miss 10 sts, cable 4 sts, crossing 2 sts at R over 2 sts at L, miss 4 sts. Repeat across knitting.
Rows 17, 18, 19 and 20: K. Col D (purple) feeder B. Miss 2 sts, cable 4 sts, crossing 2 sts at R over 2 sts at L, miss 10 sts, cable 4 sts, crossing 2 sts at L over 2 sts at R, miss 4 sts. Repeat across knitting.

Rows 21, 22, 23 and 24: K. Col E (rust) feeder B. Miss 4 sts, cable 4 sts, crossing 2 sts at R over 2 sts at L, miss 6 sts, cable 4 sts, crossing 2 sts at L over 2 sts at R, miss 6 sts. Repeat across knitting.
Rows 25, 26, 27 and 28: K col F (mustard) feeder B. Miss 6 sts, cable 4 sts, crossing 2 sts at R over 2 sts at L, miss 2 sts, cable 4 sts, crossing 2 sts at L over 2 sts at R, miss 8 sts. Repeat across knitting.
Rows 29, 30, 31 and 32: K. Col G (green) feeder B. Miss 6 sts, cable 4 sts, crossing 2 sts at L over 2 sts at R, miss 2 sts, cable 4 sts, crossing 2 sts at R over 2 sts at L, miss 8 sts.
Repeat across knitting.
This forms complete pattern from *.

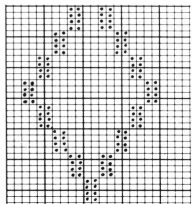

Right: UNRAVELLING DIAMONDS CABLE

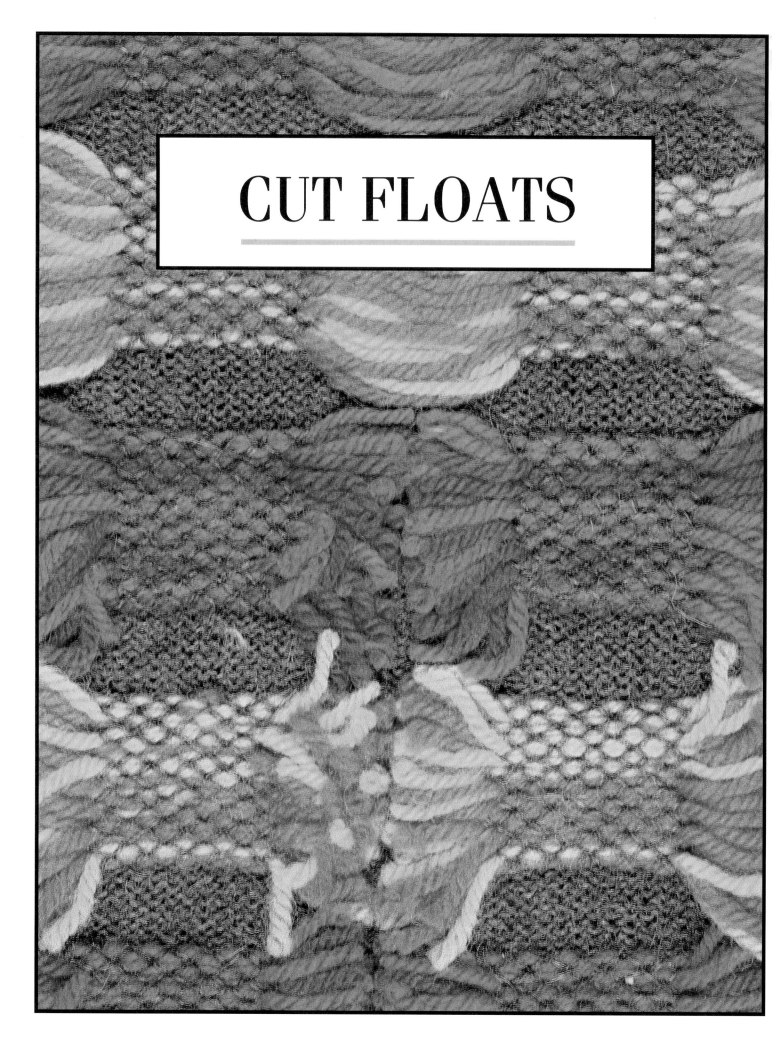

CUT FLOATS

Cut floats is a technique of cutting the long or short floats of yarn created in some knitting stitches. Weaving and jacquard provide the most scope for float cutting. To obtain the best results, it is important to plan ahead, arranging the design so that the floats formed in it produce the most effective results when cut.

When cutting floats on weaving and jacquard designs, longer floats than usual can be tolerated. It must be remembered in the case of jacquard, that when the floats are to be used for cutting, the reverse of the fabric becomes the face side.

Floats can be cut through the centre, giving an even fringe or pile, depending on how long the float is. They can be cut very close to one side making an unbalanced fringe. In jacquard designs, the floats can be totally cut away leaving only a tiny halo fringe around the design shapes and creating a much lighter fabric than usual. By experimenting, the knitter will discover the many ways in which this technique can be used and exploited.

The one rule to follow is that floats must be secured firmly. In the case of jacquards there is no problem, because the yarn is knitted between each float and so is tightly held by the forming of stitches. In weaving patterns the yarn is not knitted, only trapped behind stitches, so it is important to have enough holding stitches to secure the floats when cut. Usually 3 stitches is the minimum. The yarns used are important: wool, because of its hairiness is excellent for holding the floats, but silky yarns like rayon can present problems. It is easy to discover by experimentation which combination of yarns works best. A light wash will help to give the wool more grip when used in combination with other yarns.

Included in this section are examples of cut-float designs which have been milled. Milling is another word for felting or, as the Americans say, boiling. (For a description of how to mill fabrics, refer to the introductory section of Tuck Stitch.) Many different yarns have been used in a variety of combinations to illustrate the enormous possibilities of the cut-floats and milling technique. Readers should use this information as a stimulus towards creating innovative ideas and designs of their own. Once the technique is understood, always look carefully on the reverse side of any jacquard designs. This may inspire a second design idea based on the floats created being cut. Many of the cut float designs have been photographed to show the fringes hanging in the natural direction, although the swatch as knitted is actually on its side.

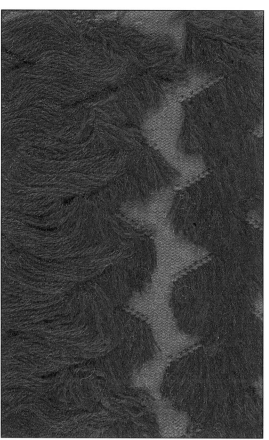

ZIG-ZAG FRINGE Version I

ZIG-ZAG FRINGE

Multiples of 24/Tension 5

Version I

100% Wool

Set for Fair Isle, insert PC.
K with col A (pink) feeder A; col B and C (blue and purple) feeder B.

When finished, the floats are cut along the line of the zig-zag. Take care to follow the pattern. To finish, trim all fringes to same length. The illustration shows the sample before and after cutting. Brush fringe with a dog brush.

Version II

Cotton and rabbit hair wool

The same design with col A (yellow cotton) feeder A; col B (rabbit hair wool) feeder B.

When knitted, the floats are cut as in version I, then the fringes are trimmed to produce the effect illustrated.

Version III

Cotton lurex and fine wool

The same design with col A (cotton and lurex) feeder A; col B (fine wool) feeder B using ¾ ends together.

When knitted, the floats are cut as in version I and then the whole sample is washed in a standard automatic washing-machine at 60°F (15°C) to mill the wool. Not illustrated.

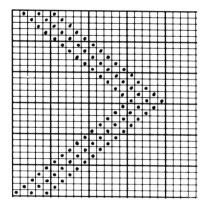

INDIAN RAG RUG

Multiples of 12/Tension 5/6
Cotton yarn and ripped silk fabric

This design uses the ordinary weaving technique, except ripped silk fabric is used instead of yarn. Col A (blue) feeder A.
Lay ripped silk by hand across needles rather than using weaving yarn guide.

The silk fabric used for this was the cheapest available, dyed in saucepans over a kitchen stove to get good colours. Any fabric which drapes well and is not too thick could be used. Try a printed patterned fabric ripped up.

The strips should be about ½in (13mm) wide; any wider and there could be trouble knitting it in.

The colour sequence here is quite random but could be knitted in a regular order.

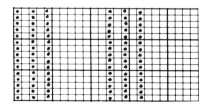

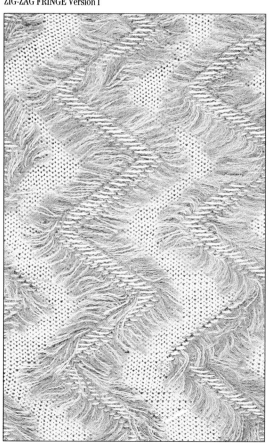

ZIG-ZAG FRINGE Version II

Right: INDIAN RAG RUG

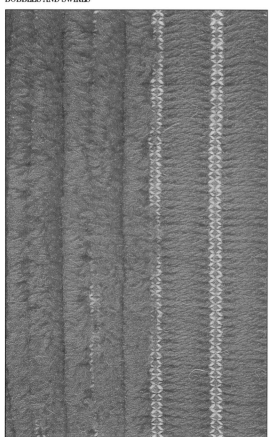

BOBBLES AND SWIRLS

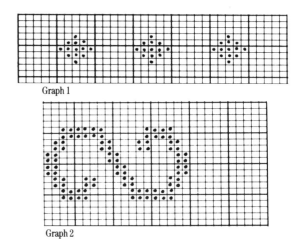

BOBBLES AND SWIRLS

Multiples of 10 and 29/Tension 8
100% Cotton chenille

The graphs for this design are worked manually.

*K 4 rows col A (maroon), change to col B (navy), K 3 rows. Pick up loops of the 1st row knitted in col B and hook these onto the needles in work. This forms a tuck. Repeat from * 3 more times (4 repeats). Turn knitting around using a garter bar or by hand. The reverse side of the knitting now faces you. Make diamond tufts using graph 1: K 3 rows col A. Push needles forward where indicated on graph and holding a ruler under and close to the needle bed, wrap col C (dark green) over the 1st selected needle, down behind ruler, under and up in front of ruler, so forming a loop. Repeat this across knitting on every selected needle. K 1 row col A. Repeat until diamond is complete as in graph.

K 3 rows col A.* Turn knitting around using a garter bar or by hand as before and knit first sequence from * to * exactly as before. When this is complete, turn knitting around once more, using garter bar or by hand. K 4 rows col B, then make loops around ruler as before following graph 2 and K 1 row col B after each row of loops. End pattern with 4 rows of col B. This sequence forms the complete repeat.

This could be used as a border only and the body of the fabric or garment could be knitted in 2 colours with tucks. The illustration shows tucks as they come off the machine and also what they look like if sewn together (smocked) after completion.

You could move the graphs around within the pattern repeats to produce your own version of this design.

Graph 1

Graph 2

CUT VELVET

Multiples of 8/Tension 7
Shetland main yarn, chunky wool weaving yarn

Col A (yellow wool) feeder A, 2 ends of col B (pink chunky) weaving yarn guide. K as PC.

100% chunky wool gives the best results. The cut floats of this yarn give a marvellously rich pile fabric. The cutting is carried out down the centre of each group of floats. The fabric is shown before and after cutting.

TUFTS AND SMOCKING

Multiples of 10/Tension 9
Maroon chenille main yarn and wool tufting

**K 3 rows col A (maroon). Following the graph, push the needles forward where marked and with col C (dark green wool), take yarn over the needle and, with an ordinary ruler held close to and under the needle bed, wrap the yarn around this by taking it down the back of the ruler, around and up the front, hook the yarn over same needle or move onto next needle depending on graph. Leaving the ruler in position, K 1 row col A. Carefully remove ruler and repeat this sequence until the pattern is complete. K 3 rows col A. You now have tufts of loops in diamond shapes on the kitting. With garter bar, or by hand, turn knitting around so the reverse side is facing you.* K 3 rows col B (navy). Pick up loops of the 1st row of sts knitted in col B and hook them back onto needles in work (this forms a tuck). K 4 rows col A and repeat from * 3 more times.

Turn the knitting around using garter bar or by hand as before so tufts are now facing again. Repeat from **.

To finish, cut the loops made in wool to form tufts in the shape of diamonds. The tucks are stitched together using a contrast colour to form smocking. You could join the tucks together any way you like to produce other designs.

Before smocking, the tucks are shown at the bottom of the swatch.

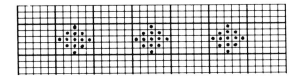

TUFTS AND SMOCKING

JACQUARD SQUARE FRINGES

Multiples of 24/Tension 7

Version I
100% wool

Set for Fair Isle, insert PC.
Col A (brown) feeder A.
Col B (tweed and beige) feeder B (2 ends).
Knit.

Version II
Acrylic and 100% wool

*Col A (navy acrylic) feeder A throughout.
Col B (red) feeder B. K 14 rows.
Col C (green) feeder B. K 14 rows.
Col D (yellow) feeder B. K 14 rows.
Col E (blue) feeder B. K 14 rows.
Repeat from *.

By running 2 ends of yarn in feeder B together, the floats are doubled and so make a much thicker fringe. A slightly quilted effect is achieved in the jacquard patterned squares.

Many variations are possible by changing colours and yarn.

The samples have been milled (see introduction to section on Tuck Stitch (page 9) for instruction on milling).

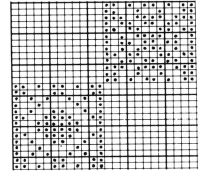

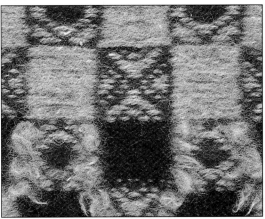

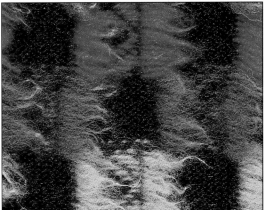

JACQUARD SQUARE FRINGES   Top: Version I   Above: Version II

SEA URCHIN

Multiples of 24/Tension 8
Rayon main yarn and wool pattern

Set for Fair Isle, insert PC.
K rayon feeder A; wool feeder B.

It is important that the yarn in
feeder A is one which will not mill
or felt. For guidance, read section
in introduction for Tuck Stitch.

Many developments stem from
this pattern.

Illustrated here are Version I
the sample as it comes off the
machine, Version II the sample
when it has been milled but floats
left uncut and Version III the sample where the floats were cut and
then the fabric was milled.

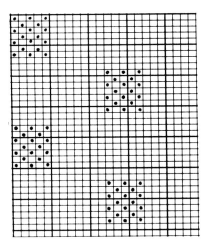

SEA URCHIN Version I

RUGS

Multiples of 24/Tension 7
4-ply Wool main yarn and chunky
wool for weaving yarn

Colour sequence as illustrated.
MC (grey) throughout.
K 15 rows with 2 ends of chunky
yarn weaving yarn guide, 1 of col
B (yellow) and 1 of col C (pink).
K 8 rows col A only.
K 15 rows with 2 ends of chunky
yarn weaving yarn guide, 1 of col
D (blue) and 1 of col E (green).

The floats are cut down the
centre of each set to create the

effect illustrated. If you wish,
the fringe can be trimmed
or shortened.

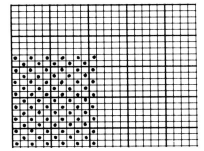

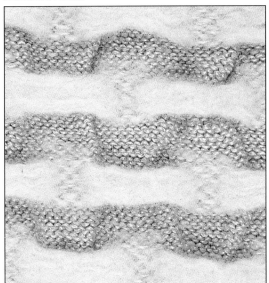

SEA URCHIN Version II

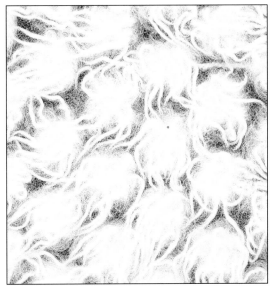

SEA URCHIN Version III

Left: RUGS

135

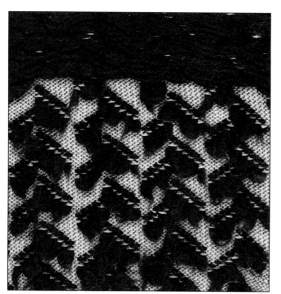

FRINGED DASH

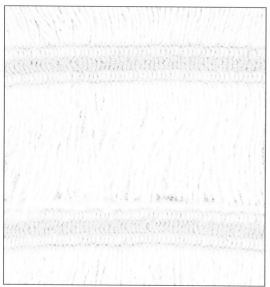

STRIPE FRINGES

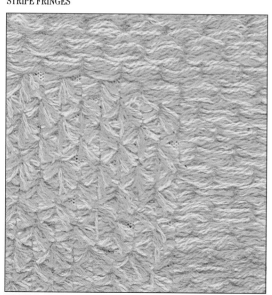

FRINGED CHECK

FRINGED DASH

Multiples of 24/Tension 5
Mercerised cotton and wool

Set for Fair Isle, insert PC.
Col A (grey cotton) feeder A; cols
B and C (green and black wool)
feeder B. Knit. When sample is big
enough, cast off.

The sample illustrated has
been milled (felted). For milling,
see introduction to section on
Tuck Stitch (page 9). The knitting
is shown before and after cutting.

The design is also very pretty un-
milled.

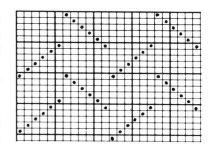

STRIPE FRINGES

Multiples of 24/Tension 6
Cotton main yarn and wool fringe

Set for Fair Isle, insert PC.
Knit jacquard as graph col A (yellow cotton) feeder A; col B (white
wool) feeder B.

Knit as ordinary jacquard until
you have the required size. Cast
off.

Press sample flat and cut floats
as near to line of holding sts as
possible, on right side. This gives
a fringed fabric. To make the

fringe full, use more than 1 end of
yarn in feeder B. This sample has
2 ends run together, but more
could be used.

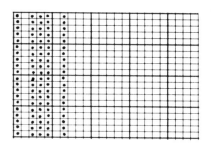

FRINGED CHECK

Multiples of 24/Tension 3-4
Mohair and acrylic

Set for Fair Isle, insert PC.
Knit jacquard as in graph, col A
(white) feeder A; cols B and C
(green and blue) feeder B.

This gives a wonderfully thick
but not heavy fabric and presents
many opportunities for development, both in colour and finish.

If this was knitted with 100%
wool in feeder B and the fabric
was milled (felted), the floats
could be made so that when they

were cut they formed small felt
flaps instead of a fringe.

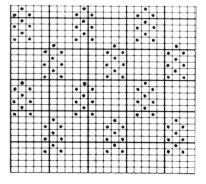

TASSEL SQUARES

Multiples of 24/Tension 6
Orange Shetland col A, feeder A
multicoloured acrylic col B,
feeder B

This small jacquard square is an
ideal design where the floats produced on the reverse side of the
design can be used to create a
wonderfully rich fabric.

K in the usual way. When finished
the reverse side becomes the
front of the fabric. Press the knitting, straightening out the floats,
then cut the floats along the right
side of each square.

Now carefully brush floats with
a dog or teasel brush. It is important to brush carefully, especially
if acrylic yarn is used, as you can
tear the ends of the yarn, and, by
doing so, lose some of the length
of the fringe. The results are a
luxurious fringed fabric.

Alternatively, 2 ends of yarn
could be used in feeder B to produce a thicker float and hence a
thick bushy fringe, or 3 ends
could be used, each one being a
different yarn. Wool and acrylic
give the best effects.

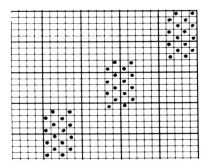

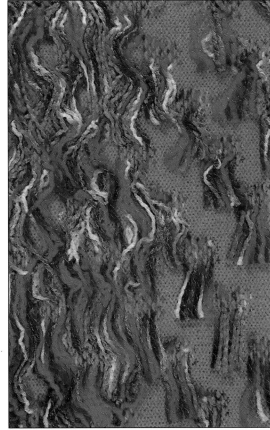

TASSEL SQUARES

STRAIGHT FRINGE

Multiples of 24/Tension 5

Version I

Cotton main yarn with multi-fibre
fine yarns for fringe

Set for Fair Isle, insert PC.
K as in graph with col A (cotton)
feeder A and col B (multi-fine
yarns) feeder B.

This demonstrates the way to
knit a straight fringe.

When the floats are cut, the fabric is used on its side if the effect
of a conventional fringe is required.

Version II

Multiples of 12
100% Wool

The number of sts between the
pattern stripe has been halved.

This gives a smaller fringe and demonstrates how simple it is to
alter the fringe size. Different
length floats used in one design
will give a variety of fringes when
cut. The colours in the 2 feeders
have also been reversed every 6
rows.

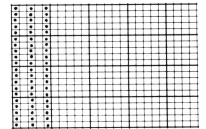

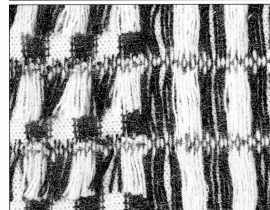

STRAIGHT FRINGE   Top: Version I   Above: Version II

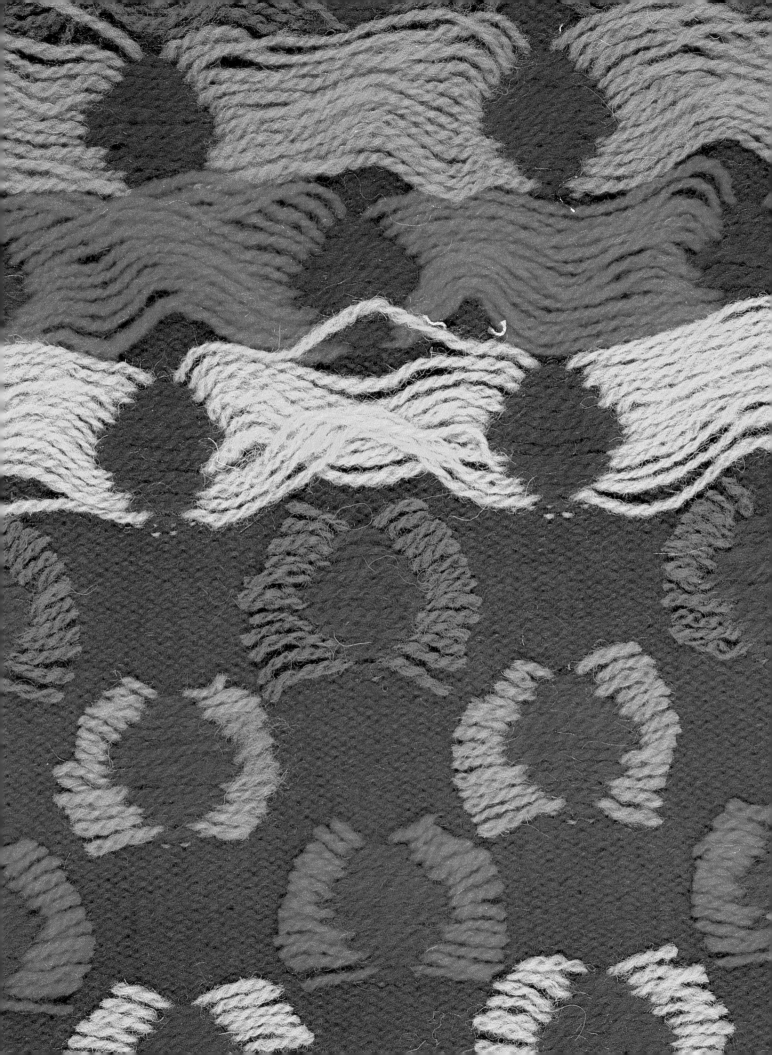

FRINGED CIRCLES

Multiples of 24/Tension 4
Shetland wool

Version I

Set for Fair Isle, insert PC.
*Col A (blue) feeder A throughout.
Col B (yellow) feeder B. Knit.
Colour in feeder B changes each
repeat of a circle in the following
order: red, orange, green. Repeat
from *.

Version II

K PC with black feeder A; green
and blue feeder B.

In this version (not illustrated)
there is no colour changing, but 2
ends of Shetland are used as one
on a slightly looser tension. This
makes the fringe thicker and look
richer.

There are many ways this design
could be developed: try cutting
the floats in different ways or
milling a sample after cutting.

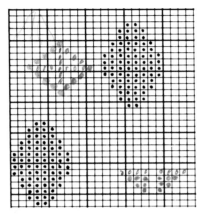

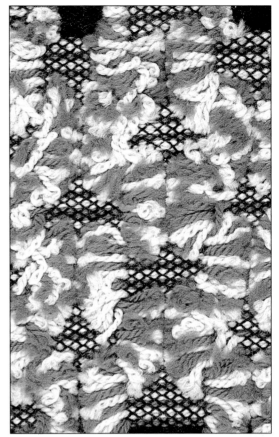

CHUNKY CHEQUER BOARD

CHUNKY CHEQUER BOARD

Multiples of 24/Tension 7
Shetland wool main yarn and
chunky wool weaving yarn

This design uses the ordinary
weaving technique.
*K 2 rows as graph with col A
(black) feeder A; col B (light
grey) used double feeder B.
K 2 rows col A feeder A; col C
(dark grey) used double feeder B.
Repeat from *.

If a variety of colour in chunky
weaving yarn is used, they could
be introduced in different sequences, creating a very exciting
multicolour fabric.

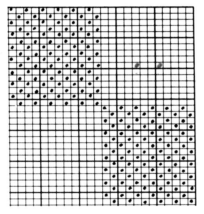

LARGE AND SMALL FRINGE

Multiples of 24/Tension 4-5
Acrylic and wool

Set for Fair Isle and insert PC.
Knit jacquard as in graph, col A
(blue) feeder A; cols B and C
(purple and black) feeder B.

K until the required size is
reached. In this design 2 ends of
4-ply are used in feeder B with 1
end in feeder A. This is to get a
rich thick fringe. In the sample, 2
colours are used in feeder B. You

could change this to stripes or
make it all solid colour.
Try your own variations.

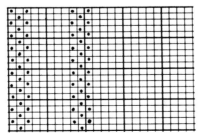

LARGE AND SMALL FRINGE

Left: FRINGED CIRCLES Version I

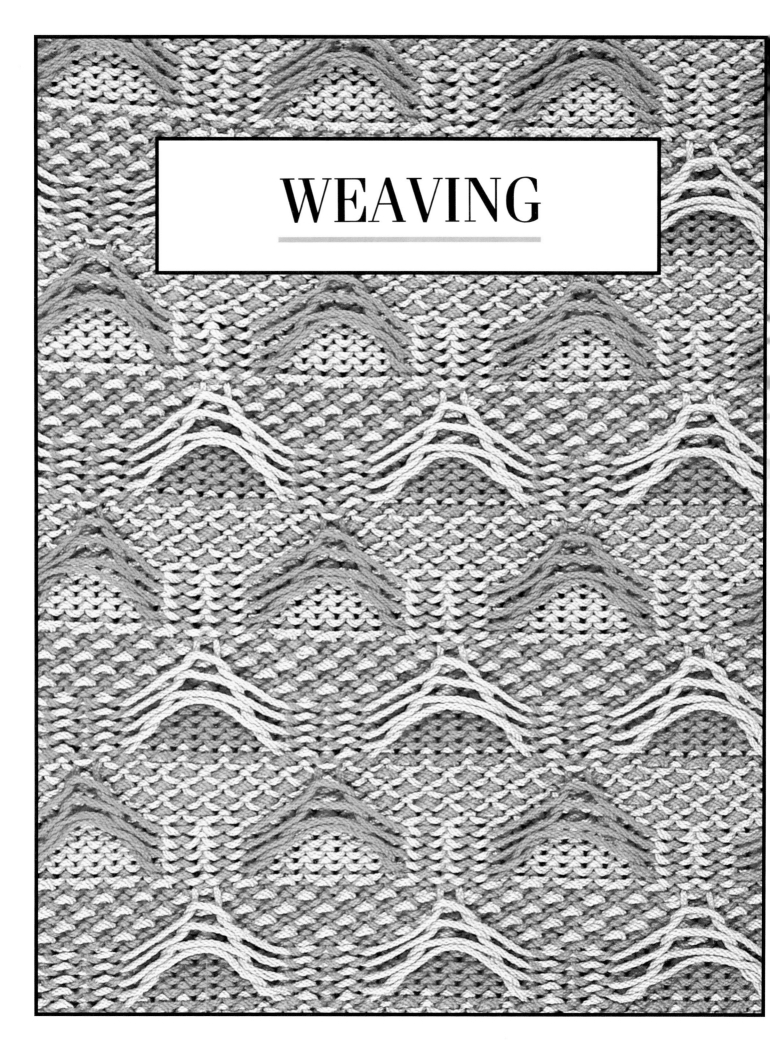

WEAVING

Weaving is one of the most attractive of single-bed techniques; it is also one of the most versatile. The technique consists of an extra yarn being woven into the stitches on the reverse side of a fabric, without ever being knitted itself. This allows the use of yarn which normally would be too thick or too textured to be knitted. The technique will be described in your machine manual; refer to this before starting.

Basically, weaving is knitted as follows. Programme your punchcard or graph pattern into the machine, feed your main yarn into the yarn carriage in the normal way and place the weaving yarn in the weaving-yarn guide, always in front of the carriage, whichever way it is moving. At the end of each row, remove the weaving yarn manually from its guide and insert it into the guide on the opposite side of the carriage. Weaving can also be worked by hand, the weaving yarn being laid across the knitting needles by hand, rather than by the yarn carriage. This is called 'laying in' and can be useful for particularly heavy textured yarns.

In this section, I have demonstrated the versatility of this technique by different stitches, and how the floats can also be cut and used to create pile fabrics or fringe decoration. Any yarn, up to heavy chunky, can be used for weaving. The thicker the yarn the more care is needed at the start, and until you are familiar with the feel of the technique, it is sensible to move the carriage with a little care across the knitting. The fabrics produced from weaving have little stretch across their width, but are firm and ideal for cut-and-sew garments, as well as for more conventionally fashioned ones.

It is useful with any weaving-in pattern to experiment with it by using different types of yarns for both the main colour and the weaving or laying in. By combining weaving with other techniques, such as jacquard or lace, wonderful textured and patterned fabrics can be produced.

IKAT CHEVRON

Multiples of 8/Tension 6
100% Cotton

*K 8 rows col A (green) feeder A; col B weaving yarn guide.
Now pick up lowest float and put onto needle 5 in every set of 8 across work.
K 1 row col A feeder A; nothing weaving yarn guide. Pick up lowest float and put onto needle 5 in every set of 8. Repeat until all 8 floats have been hooked up.
K 8 rows col A feeder A; col C weaving yarn guide.
Now hook lowest float onto needle 1 in every set of 8 across work.
K 1 row col A feeder A; nothing in weaving yarn guide. Hook lowest float onto needle 1. Repeat until all floats have been hooked up across the knitting. Repeat from *.

This is a 32 row repeat.
To knit the design illustrated, change colour in weaving yarn guide every 1st 8 rows in the repeat of 16.

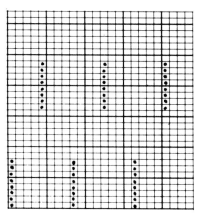

DOT STITCH

DOT STITCH

Multiples of 2/Tension 8
Shetland wool

K as graph: col A feeder A; col B weaving yarn guide.

This is a useful stitch to use in one garment with jacquards or other more decorative stitches. Many different interpretations can be made by the imaginative use of fancy yarns and colour.

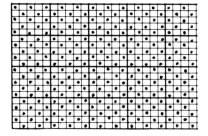

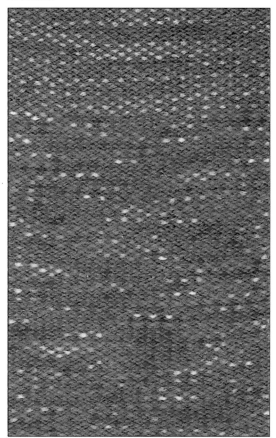
DOT STITCH

Left: IKAT CHEVRON

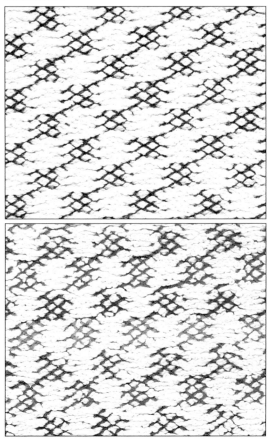

DIAMOND ROPE

DIAMOND ROPE

Multiples of 12/Tension 4-5
Acrylic with chunky wool weaving yarn

This design will lend itself to interpretation in any colour and the weaving yarn can be any thick chunky yarn. Experiment with striping colour into the background pattern and by using a really chunky bobble fancy yarn for the weaving. Think also of using tweed or multicolour yarns.

*K 13 rows acrylic, then lay chunky yarn over selected needles.
K 12 rows, then with transfer tool, pick up loops of weaving yarn and hook over selected needles. Repeat from *.

If your machine does not pre-select the needles marked on row 13, bring forward manually and then lay weaving yarn over them. Repeat the manual selection on row 25, then pick up loops of weaving yarn from row 13. Repeat this sequence for each repeat of the pattern.

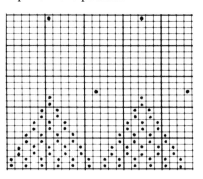

CHESS BOARD

Multiples of 8/Tension 8
4-ply Wool main yarn; chunky cotton chain, weaving yarn

Version I
K as graph with wool feeder A and chunky cotton chain weaving yarn guide.

Version II
K as Version I, but change the main yarn feeder A every 6 rows.

An interesting colour effect can be achieved by changing the colour in the weaving yarn guide for the last and first rows of each square.

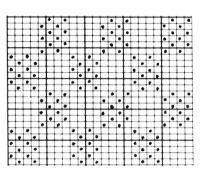

CHESS BOARD   Top: Version I   Above: Version II

INLAID TUCK

Multiples of 24/Tension 6-7
100% Cotton with cords of rayon and lurex

The main design is a simple tuck as shown in the graphs knitted in one colour. The weaving in of the tubes is as follows:
Row 12: lay over each selected needle (the 1st cord of col B (lurex)) leaving it looped.
Row 18: lay over each selected needle the 2nd cord col C (pink cotton) leaving it looped.
Row 22: pick up 1st cord loop and hook this over each selected needle.
Row 28: pick up 2nd cord loop and hook this over every selected needle.
All other rows are knitted. This is a 29 row repeat.

If your machine does not select needles on the row before the one you are about to knit, these needles will have to be selected manually, according to the graph.

Many variations can be knitted. A very rich effect is produced if the tuck stitch is striped with colours of close tones over which contrasting cords are inlaid.

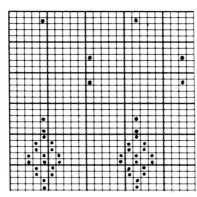

INLAID TUCK

DIAMOND EYELET

Multiples of 8/Tension 7
Mercerised cotton main yarn and rayon weaving yarn

*K 4 rows col A (natural cotton) feeder A; col B (pink rayon) weaving yarn guide.
K 4 rows col A, feeder A; nothing weaving yarn guide.
Transfer the stitch from needle 5 onto needle 4 and the stitch from needle 7 onto needle 8 in every set of 8 needles across the knitting. Now hook floats made with col B onto needle 2. Centre needle between transfers.
K 4 rows col A, feeder A; col B weaving yarn guide.
K 4 rows col A, feeder A; nothing weaving yarn guide.
Transfer the stitch from needle 3 onto needle 4 and the stitch from needle 1 onto needle 8 in every set of 8 needles across the

knitting.
Now hook floats made with col B onto needle 6. Centre needle between transfers.
Repeat from *.

Two versions of this design are illustrated. The lower half shows the knitting as it comes off the machine. The upper half has a chunky rayon yarn threaded through the holes made by transferring the stitches. A little imagination in the use of colour could also enhance this design further.

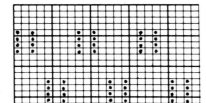

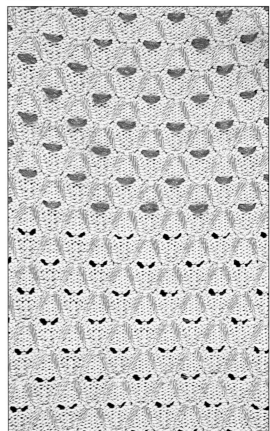

DIAMOND EYELET

BUTTERFLY

Multiples of 12/Tension 7
Shetland wool main yarn and ribbon tape for weaving

*K 5 rows col A (Shetland wool); col B (ribbon tape) weaving yarn guide.
K 5 rows col A.
Now hook up floats onto needle 5, marked X on graph.
K 5 rows col A; col B weaving yarn guide.
K 5 rows col A.
Now hook up floats onto needle 11, marked X on graph.
Repeat from *.

Although at first this stitch is slow to produce, with experience the knitting grows quicker. The end results are worth any amount of patience.

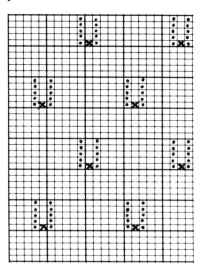

ZEBRA CROSSING

Multiples of 24/Tension 3
3-ply Mixture of mohair and wool

K as graph: col A (black) feeder A; col B (white) weaving yarn guide.

A classic diagonal stripe.
A great feature could be made of the stripes if they are used imaginatively when planning a garment.

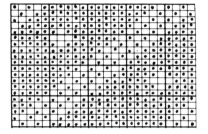

ZEBRA CROSSING

TAPED STRIPE

Multiples of 12/Tension 8
Shetland and rayon

K as graph. Col A (dark green Shetland) feeder A; col B (beige rayon ribbon) weaving yarn guide.
    The rayon tape with its wonderful shine, looks very good against the matt wool and gives a rich expensive look to this pattern.

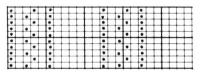

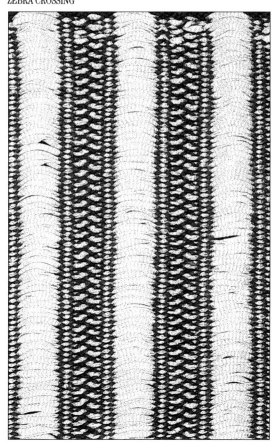

TAPED STRIPE

Right: BUTTERFLY

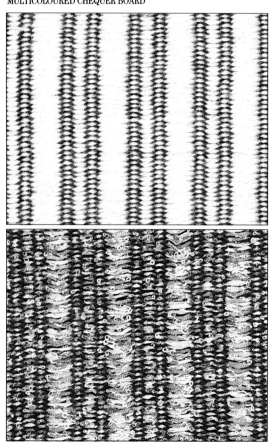

MULTICOLOURED CHEQUER BOARD

MULTICOLOURED CHEQUER BOARD

Multiples of 12/Tension 8
Shetland wool with acrylic
multicolour

Col A (purple Shetland) feeder A.

Unlike the other weaving patterns, this one needs a separate end of yarn and colour for each set of needles to be woven over – ie, every set of 8 needles. If you use a machine which does not push out selected needles into UWP, you must do this manually. Now with separate balls or ends of yarn, lay a separate colour over each set of 8 needles allowing the ends to hang down. K 1 row normally. Repeat this from the opposite side. Lay the weaving yarn over the set of 8 needles as before. K 1 row.

This is repeated 10 times until the sets of 8 selected needles change. At this point, take the weaving yarn across the knitting onto the nearest set of 8 needles and lay it across as before. K 1 row and repeat 10 times. This is the pattern.

When the position of the needles changes every 10 rows, a loop is formed that gives the surface added interest. Great richness can be achieved with this design by using contrasting colours. By using separate balls or ends, every square could be a different colour if you wish.

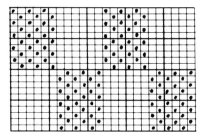

RAILWAY

Multiples of 8/Tension 7
4-ply Wool with chunky wool
weaving yarn

Version I
K as graph. Col A (dark green) feeder A; col B (cream chunky) weaving yarn guide.

Version II
K as graph. Col A (navy) feeder A; col B (multicoloured rayon tape with acrylic loop) weaving yarn guide .

Stripes could be worked into this design both in the main yarn and in the weaving yarn. Different colours combined would produce an extremely rich and interesting fabric. Try mixing the textured yarns used for weaving.

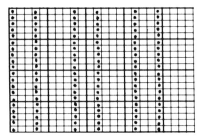

RAILWAY   Top: Version I   Above: Version II

HEARTS AND ZIG-ZAG

Multiples of 24/Tension 5
Lambswool and acrylic

*K 17 rows col A (green).
Set for weaving and insert PC.
K 6 rows col A feeder A, col B (white) weaving yarn guide.
K 8 rows col A; no yarn weaving yarn guide.
K 17 rows col A feeder A; col C (rust) weaving yarn guide.
K 8 rows col A; no yarn weaving yarn guide.
K 6 rows col A feeder A; col D (yellow) weaving yarn guide.
K 8 rows col A; no yarn weaving yarn guide.
K 17 rows col A feeder A; col C weaving yarn guide.
K 8 rows col A; no yarn weaving yarn guide.
Repeat from *.

The right side of the fabric is used, the reverse of that normally used in weaving designs (see Jacquard Hearts below). By using the face of the fabric, a very subtle pattern is seen, which can be emphasised by outlining some of the shapes with chain stitch (see illustration).

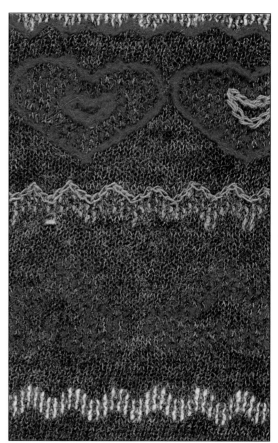

HEARTS AND ZIG-ZAG

JACQUARD HEARTS

Multiples of 24/Tension 6
Lambswool

*Insert PC as above for Hearts and Zig-Zag and K with col A (green) feeder A throughout.
K 17 rows col B (cream) weaving yarn guide. The weaving yarn must always be in front of the carriage, whichever way it is moving.
Remove col B, K 8 rows col A.
Place col B weaving yarn guide, K 6 rows.
Remove col B, K 8 rows col A.
Place col B weaving yarn guide, K 17 rows.
Remove col B, K 8 rows col A.

Place col B weaving yarn guide, K 6 rows.
Remove col B, K 8 rows. Repeat from *.

To finish, wash in pure soap (using an automatic washing-machine on light wash). This felts the wool; you can now cut the floats away revealing the design of hearts. The fabric can be felted by hand if you have no washing-machine; use very little hot water, pure soap flakes and rub vigorously.

The reason for the felting is to prevent movement when the floats are cut.

JACQUARD HEARTS

149

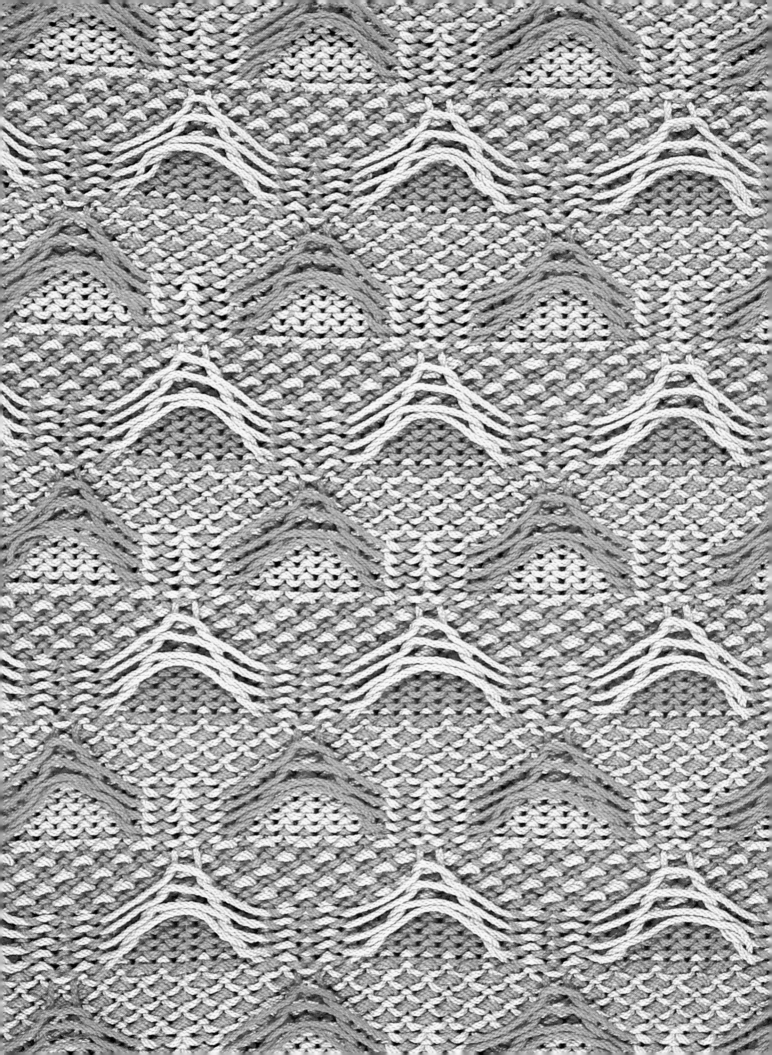

EIFFEL TOWER

Multiples of 12/Tension 6
100% Cotton perle

Set for Fair Isle, insert PC.
*K 10 rows col A (green) feeder A;
col B (rust) weaving yarn guide.

Latch up floats as if picking up a dropped stitch and hook final float onto needle marked X on graph.

K 10 rows col A feeder A; col B weaving yarn guide.

Latch up floats and hook final float onto needle marked X.
Repeat from *.

This is a beautiful stitch that can be greatly enhanced by experimenting with textured yarns in the weaving yarn guide. Any type of yarn can be tried.

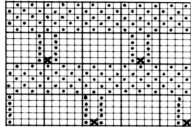

DIAMOND QUILT

Multiples of 12/Tension 8
Shetland wool

Version I
K as graph. Col A (orange) feeder A; col B (blue) weaving yarn guide.

Versions II and III
K as Version I, but in fancy textured yarns – ie, pink chenille on wool and bright pink mohair on

wool. Alternatively, change the colour of the weaving yarn every complete repeat of the punchcard.

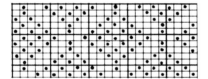

DIAMOND QUILT Version I

DIAMOND QUILT Version II

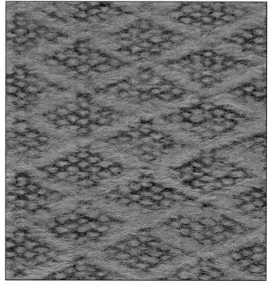

DIAMOND QUILT Version III

Left: EIFFEL TOWER

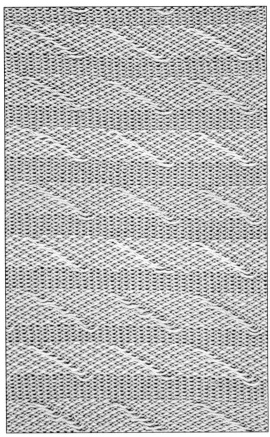

DASHES AND STRIPES Version I

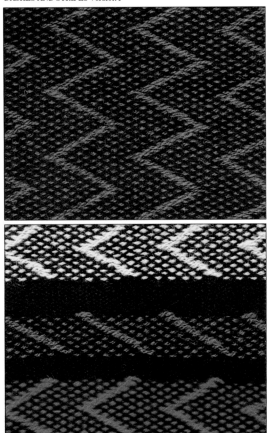

BIRD'S-EYE ZIG-ZAG   Top: Version I   Above: Version II

DASHES AND STRIPES

Multiples of 12/Tension 6
100% Cotton

This pattern can be knitted 2 ways. Version I is illustrated.

Version I
Set for Fair Isle, insert PC.
*K 8 rows col A (grey) feeder A; col B (pink) weaving yarn guide.
K 6 rows col A feeder A only, keeping pattern card running.
K 8 rows col A feeder A; col C (lilac) weaving yarn guide.

K 6 rows col A feeder A only.
Keep pattern card running.
Repeat from *.

Version II
Insert a small jacquard pattern between the weaving pattern.

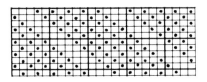

BIRD'S-EYE ZIG-ZAG

Multiples of 24/Tension 6-7
Shetland wool

This zig-zag design can be interpreted in many ways.
Two are illustrated here.

Version I
To knit, follow graph.
Col A (black) feeder A; col B (green) weaving yarn guide.

Version II
This is a random colour sequence. The punchcard revolves continuously, but coloured yarn is not always put in the weaving yarn guide. This creates plain stripes

between 2 coloured blocks where weaving yarn has been used. Make up your own design or follow this one. By using the weaving yarn guide randomly, the zig-zag pattern is broken up. More versions of this pattern could be created using this technique.

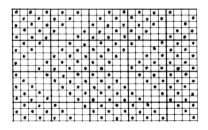

CORNFIELD

Multiples of 12/Tension 6
Cotton main yarn and rayon weaving yarn

*K 8 rows col A (sand) feeder A; col B (turquoise) weaving yarn guide.
K 6 rows col A feeder A; col C (natural) weaving yarn guide.
Repeat from *.

The design is shown as it comes off the machine with floats uncut and also with the floats cut. The two different effects can be used separately or together in one garment. To cut floats, iron fabric first, then with sharp scissors cut through the centre of each set of 8.

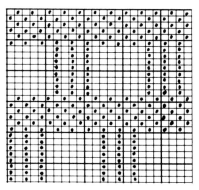

CORNFIELD

WINDOW PANE

Multiples of 24/Tension 3
3-ply Mohair/wool mixture

K as graph. Col A (black) feeder A; col B (white) weaving yarn guide.
A very understated check, the introduction of colour could radically change this design if it was thought out carefully.

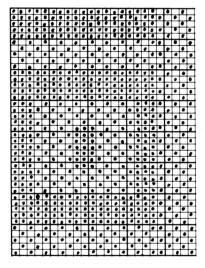

WINDOW PANE

DIAMOND CHECK

Multiples of 24/Tension 8
Shetland wool main yarn and chenille weaving yarn

This design has a good soft velvety feel and look. This is achieved by using chenille as the weaving yarn.

To knit, follow graph with col A (Shetland wool) feeder A; col B (chenille) weaving yarn guide.

By experimenting with colour and texture this could be turned into a rich design similar to a Persian carpet.

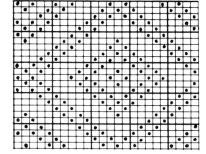

DIAMOND CHECK

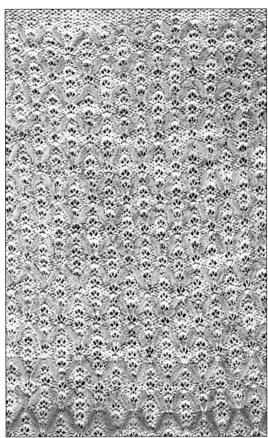

RIPPLES

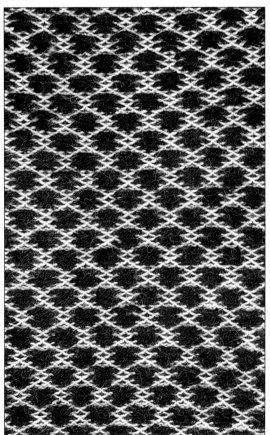

OPTIC

FRINGES AND WEAVING

Multiples of 12/Tension 5
Lambswool and fine rayon twist yarn

* K 6 rows col A (white).
K 2 rows col B (rust), then transfer every 3rd st to next needle on left.
K 2 rows col B.
Change to col A, K 6 rows.
Set for weaving and insert PC.
Col C (grey) feeder A; col A weaving yarn guide. K 7 rows PC.
Set for normal knitting. K 6 rows col A.
K 2 rows col B. Transfer every 3rd st to next needle on L. K 2 rows.
Change to col A, K 26 rows. Trans-fer every alternate st to next needle on L.
Repeat from *.

To add fringe, take 2-3 ends of lambswool, thread this through holes made in white area of knitting and knot. When complete, cut all fringes the same length. This sample has been milled (felted) when it was completed, but this is optional (see note for milling).

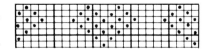

RIPPLES

Multiples of 6/Tension 5
Yarn A: 100% rayon multicolour; yarn B: 100% rayon chenille (grey)

Set for tuck.
*K 4 rows, weave with yarn B, looping the yarn over every 6th needle.
K 6 rows, then hook the loop already made onto the needle directly above – ie, every 6th needle.
This forms a zig-zag.
K 4 rows, weave with yarn B, looping the yarn over every 6th needle.

K 6 rows, then hook the loop already made onto the needle directly above. Repeat from *. This is the repeat which forms a diamond overlay.

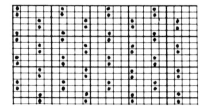

OPTIC

Multiples of 6/Tension 5
Shetland wool

This design is knitted in black and white, but there are many other ways of colouring it.

To knit, follow the graph with col A (white) feeder A; col B (black) weaving yarn guide.

A dramatic checker-board effect can be achieved by using 2 col-ours for the weaving, changing them every 6 rows.

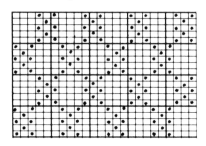

BRAIDS
AND EDGINGS

Knitted braids and edgings are among the most visually exciting forms of knitting. Many of them are easy to knit even for the beginner. Most braids are knitted on a small number of stitches (2-12). Working in such a small area stretches the designer's imagination and encourages the use of beautiful, but slow, hand techniques which might not be contemplated over larger areas, such as garment pieces.

Most braids are produced by lifting stitches off needles in different orders, dropping fancy yarns or knitted cords behind the stitch, then replacing it back on the needle. As can be seen from the designs illustrated, there are many intricate ways of arranging the textured yarns behind the needles. Once the technique has been mastered, a knitter can make up his or her own yarn combinations and designs.

Edgings are produced in a number of different ways. Those described in this section can be worked on and easily adapted to make them more personal. All the designs can be used to edge and trim a garment. Instead of using the common hem, welt or picot, these trims offer many other alternatives.

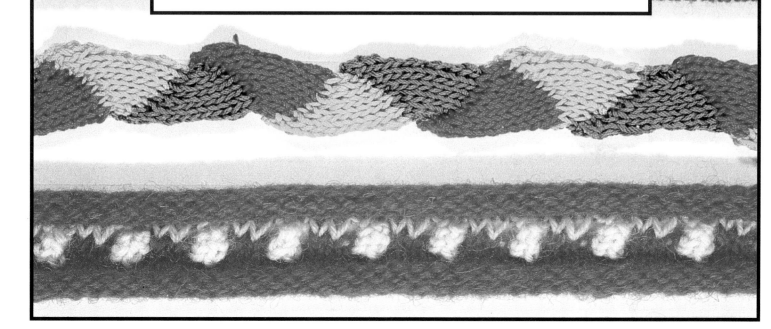

In the 1930s, 40s and 50s, Chanel the great couturier used such edging, particularly braid, to trim her now famous suits. Contemporary cardigans, jackets and skirts can be given a similarly expensive look when edged in a richly textured braid. While many of those illustrated are brightly coloured, subtle colourings in close tone knitting can look very sophisticated and tasteful.

The knitter will quickly discover that many of the designs can be incorporated into an ordinary piece of knitting, so doing away with the usual necessity of sewing them on later. Some of the most beautiful designs in this section are simple to knit, the only requisite being patience. Once a pattern has been learnt, the knitting process can become quick and interesting.

To obtain the best results when knitting edgings and braids, it is essential to experiment with different textured yarns and knitted cords. The cords can be knitted in any kind of yarn and it is fun to stripe colour into them as they are knitted. Cords can be produced in two ways:

1 Simply knit across three needles; the strip of knitting produced naturally curls into a cord.
2 Knit over three needles with the part-button (slip) on your carriage in work. This allows the carriage to knit in one direction only, producing a float in the opposite direction. This forms a tight, very compact cord.

Among the simplest designs in this section are fringes; again, experimentation will be rewarded by better results. If single ends of 4-ply yarn are used, only a thin, poor-looking fringe is produced; by knitting with more than one end of yarn, richer, thicker fringes can be achieved. Experiment with tension as well as with the number of yarn ends to be knitted.

With edgings knitted horizontally, there is a problem of limited length, as you can only knit a length the width of your machine. It is important to remember this and to plan wherever possible to use such edgings without joining them, unless you are a particularly skilled and a neat sewer.

While some designs are slow to knit, many are not, and if planned carefully and with good colouring, they can transform a garment into something special.

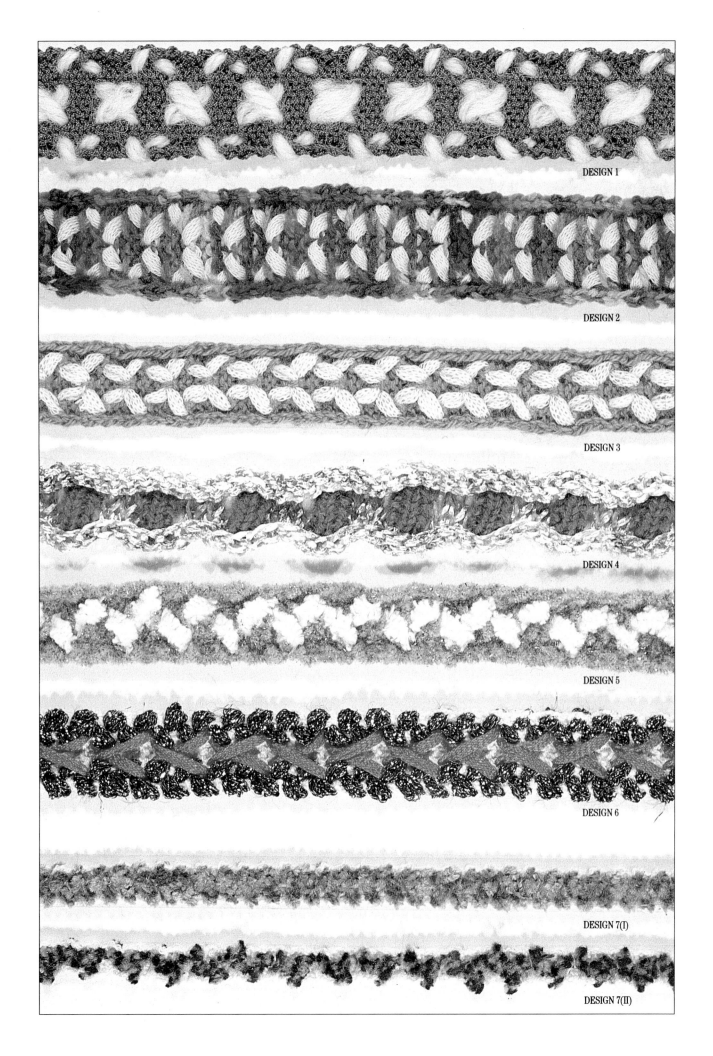

DESIGN 1

DESIGN 2

DESIGN 3

DESIGN 4

DESIGN 5

DESIGN 6

DESIGN 7(I)

DESIGN 7(II)

DESIGN 1

Tension 5
Cotton main yarn; chunky wool laying-in yarn (2 ends of same colour)

Cast on 9 sts in cotton: 1, 2, 3, 4, 5, 6, 7, 8 and 9.
K 10 rows, * then take st from needle 1 and place 1 end of col A (chunky yarn) behind st, working from R to L, replace st on needle. Take st from needle 9 and place col B (chunky yarn) behind st, working from L to R, replace st.

K 2 rows.
Take st from needle 3 and place col A behind st, working from L to R, replace st on needle.
Take st from needle 7 and place col B behind st, working R to L, replace st. K 4 rows.
Take st from needle 3 and place col B behind st, working from R to L, replace st on needle.
Take st from needle 7 and place col A behind st from L to R, replace st. K 2 rows. Repeat from *.

DESIGN 2

Tension 6
Multicolour acrylic main yarn and cotton tape yarn (2 ends)

Needle set-out 11··11··11
*K 2 rows MC.
Lift st off needle 2 and place col A (tape) behind. Replace st, lift st off needle 6 and place col B (tape) behind, replace st.

K 2 rows.
Lift st from needle 3. Place col A behind, lift st from needle 4 and place col B behind, replace st. Repeat from *.

Although cotton tape is used for inlaying here, almost any fancy yarn or knitted cord could be used.

DESIGN 3

Tension 4
Silk and cotton tape (2 ends)

Cast on 9 sts MC (blue silk).
K 6 rows. Start pattern.
*Take st from needle 3 and place tape behind st, then replace st. Repeat this on needle 7 with a 2nd length of tape.
K 2 rows.
Take st from needle 5 and place both ends of tape behind it, crossing them over L to R and R to L. The tape ends are now on opposite sides of the central needle, needle 5.
K 2 rows. Repeat from *.

This is a very simple braid and many versions can be knitted by changing yarns, textures and colours both in the main yarn and the laying-in yarn, which here is a cotton tape.

DESIGN 4

Multiples of 5/Tension 7
Rayon multicolour with wool

Cast on as many sts as you require the length of braid to be.
K 4 rows col A (rayon multicolour), carriage on R.
Push all needles into HP and set for Hold.
Push 1st 5 needles on R into WP. K 1 row col B (mauve wool). Push 1st 2 needles into HP. K 7 rows.

Carriage on R.
*Push next set of 5 needles into WP, K 1 row, col B.
Push 5 needles on R into HP. K 7 rows col B over the remaining 3 needles.
Repeat from * across the knitting. Change carriage from Hold to normal knitting and with col A, K 3 rows. Cast off with col A.

DESIGN 5

Tension 6
Needle set-out 11··11
Fine chenille

Cast on 4 sts across 6 needles as above. K 4 rows MC.
*Pull out needle 3 and lay fancy textured yarn over it.
K 2 rows, pull out needle 2, lay fancy yarn over it. K 2 rows, repeat from *.

This is a very simple braid from which many variations can be knitted. Any yarn can be used, but for the best effect the fancy yarn should be thick or chunky.

DESIGN 6

Tension 7
Cotton main yarn and gimp

This braid is made from 4 cords, tapes or fancy yarns on a background of straight yarn.
Cast on 6 sts: 1, 2, 3, 4, 5, 6. T7 for cotton gimp.
Cords A and B (black); cords C and D (pink).
K 4 rows MC.
Take st from needle 1 and place cord A behind it R to L, replace st.
Take st from needle 6 and place cord B behind it L to R, replace st.
Take st from needle 2 and place cord C behind it L to R, replace st.
Take st from needle 5 and place cord D behind it R to L, replace st.
*K 2 rows MC.
Take st from needle 2 and place cord A behind it L to R, replace st.
Take st from needle 5 and place cord B behind it R to L, replace st.
K 2 rows MC.

Take st from needle 1 and place cord A behind it R to L, replace st.
Take st from needle 6 and place cord B behind it L to R, replace st.
Take st from needle 2 and place cord D behind it R to L, replace st.
Take st from needle 5 and place cord C behind it L to R, replace st.
K 2 rows MC.
Take st from needle 2 and place cord A behind it L to R, replace st.
Take st from needle 5 and place cord B behind it R to L, replace st.
K 2 rows MC.
Take st from needle 1 and place cord A behind it R to L, replace st.
Take st from needle 6 and place cord B behind it L to R, replace st.
Take st from needle 2 and place cord C behind it L to R, replace st.
Take st from needle 5 and place cord D behind it L to R, replace st.
Repeat from *. Note cords C and D always cross each other.

DESIGN 7

Tension 6
Cotton gimp main yarn and chenille

This delicate braid can be knitted in any fancy yarn on a straight yarn.

Version I
Cast on 3 sts.
*K 1 row col A (cotton gimp).
Bring 1st needle on R forward, but be careful to keep the st over the latch. Lay col B (fancy yarn) into the hook of the needle, working from L to R.
K 1 row col A.
Bring 1st needle on L forward. Lay col B into the hook of the needle, working from R to L and repeat from *.

Version II
Work exactly as Version I but with 2 rows of knitting between laying in of fancy yarn instead of one.

DESIGN 8

DESIGN 9

DESIGN 10

DESIGN 11

DESIGN 12

DESIGN 13

DESIGN 8

Tension 10
Rowan chenille used double
Needle set-out 111⋯⋯111

Cast on 1st group of 3 sts as above, carry yarn over to 2nd 3 sts. Cast these on, then start knitting.
This forms the braid and can be worked in many other yarns.

DESIGN 9

Tension 6
4-ply wool

This braid is made from knitted cords. To make these cords, cast on 3 sts and K. A good cord can be knitted by using the part or slip buttons. This allows you to K 1 row and float across the reverse row and creates a rounder, tighter cord.

Attach the cords while knitting the braid. This is done by picking up loops from the cords and hooking them onto needles.
Cast on 8 sts MC (black) T6-7.

To start the pattern, attach the 3 cords as follows: cords A and C on R, cord B on L.
*K 4 rows MC.
Take cord A and hook this onto the last needle on the opposite side of knitting.
K 4 rows MC.
Take cord B and hook this onto the last needle on the opposite side of the knitting.
K 4 rows MC.
Take cord C and hook this onto the last needle on the opposite side of the knitting. This sequence from * forms the repeat.

DESIGN 10

Tension 5-6
Needle set-out 11·111111·11
100% Cotton

Cast on 10 sts following the needle set-out.
*K 6 rows, then cable middle 6 sts using 2 three-pronged transfer tools.
Pick up 3 sts on L of the centre block with transfer tool 1. Pick up next 3 sts on R of the centre block with transfer tool 2 and put these onto the 3 empty needles on L. Take the 3 sts from L on transfer tool 1 over the 3 sts just transferred and put these onto the 3 empty needles on R.
This is the cable. Repeat from *.

DESIGN 11

Tension 7
Shetland wool

Cast on over alternate needles in col A (pink). Length of braid is dictated by number of sts cast on. K 1 row col A, all needles in work.

Change to col B (blue), K 10 rows. Hook loops made by cast-on row onto alternate needles, K.

This edging is pretty and can be used in a variety of ways either as a trim, finish or decoration.

DESIGN 12

Tension 5
Mercerised cotton

Worked over 8 stitches
Needles numbered 1, 2, 3, 4, 5, 6, 7 and 8.
Cast on 8 sts. Set for partial knitting.
Using col A (green), carriage on R, all needles in WP, *push needle 1 into HP.
K 1 row, then loop yarn around needle 1 to prevent hole.
K 1 row.
Repeat the sequence from * with needles 2, 3, 4, 5, 6, 7 and 8.
All needles are now in HP. Take carriage to L. This forms repeat 1.

Push all needles back into WP, using col B (yellow), carriage on L, **push needle 8 into HP.
K 1 row, then loop yarn around needle 8 to prevent hole.
K 1 row.
Repeat the sequence from ** with needles 7, 6, 5, 4, 3, 2 and 1.
All needles are now in HP. Take carriage to R. This forms repeat 2.

Change to col C (pink) and follow repeat 1.
Change to col A and follow repeat 2.
Change to col B and follow repeat 1.
Change to col C and follow repeat 2.
Repeat from the beginning.

DESIGN 13

Multiples of 2/Tension 7
Shetland wool

Cast on as many sts as you require the length of braid to be.
*K 8 rows col A (pink).
Push all needles into HP and set for Hold. Change to col B (white), carriage on R.
Push 1st 4 needles on R into WP,

K 1 row. Push 1st 2 needles into HP and K 5 rows, carriage on R. Push next 4 needles into WP and K 1 row. Push 4 needles on R into HP and K 5 rows over the remaining 2 needles. Repeat from * across the knitting.
Set for normal knitting and col A. K 7 rows and cast off with col A.

DESIGN 14

Tension 3
100% Cotton

Knit 2 cords in different colours (see braid pattern 9).

Cast on 8 sts: 1, 2, 3, 4, 5, 6, 7 and 8.
K 2 rows MC (cream), then take st from needle 1 and place cord A behind the st, working from R to L. Replace st on needle, then place cord B behind the st on needle 8 in the same way, working from L to R.
K 2 rows MC, then place cord A behind st on needle 2, working from L to R, and cord B behind st on needle 7, working from R to L as row 1.
K 2 rows MC, then place cord A behind st on needle 3, working from L to R, and cord B behind st on needle 6, working from R to L as row 1.
K 2 rows MC. Place cord A behind st on needle 4, working from L to R, and cord B behind st on needle 5, working from R to L as row 1.
K 2 rows MC, then place cord A behind st on needle 5, working from L to R, and cord B behind st on needle 4, working from R to L as row 1. At this point the cords cross over.
K 2 rows MC, then place cord A behind st on needle 6, working from L to R, and cord B behind st on needle 3, working from R to L as row 1.
K 2 rows MC. Place cord A behind st on needle 7, working from L to R, and cord B behind st on needle 2, working from R to L as row 1.

This forms repeat 1. Repeat 2, which completes the pattern, is exactly the same except read cord A as cord B and read cord B as cord A.

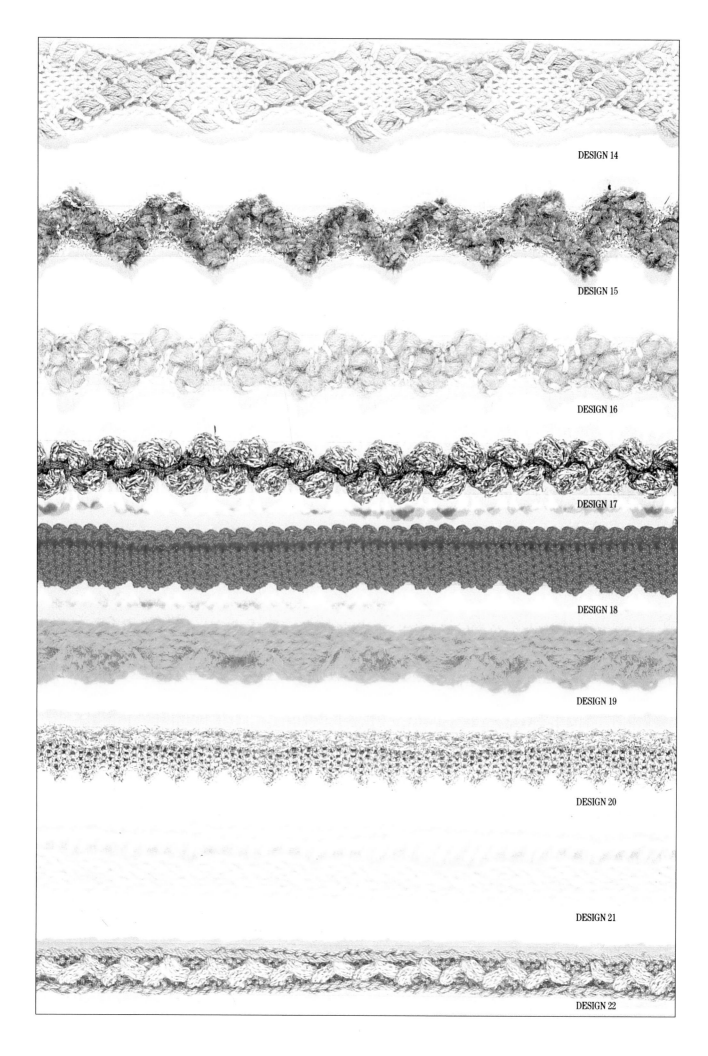

DESIGN 14

DESIGN 15

DESIGN 16

DESIGN 17

DESIGN 18

DESIGN 19

DESIGN 20

DESIGN 21

DESIGN 22

DESIGN 15

Tension 2
Lurex and 2 ends of chenille used as 1

Cast on 5 sts: 1, 2, 3, 4 and 5.
*K 1 row MC (lurex). Bring needle 1 forward, but be careful to keep the st over the latch. Lay col B (chenille) into the hook of the needle, working from R to L.
K 1 row MC, bring needle 2 forward and lay in col B, working from L to R as row 1.
K 1 row MC. Bring needle 3 forward and lay in col B, working from L to R as row 1.

K 1 row MC. Bring needle 4 forward and lay in col B, working from L to R as row 1.
K 1 row MC. Bring needle 5 forward and lay in col B, working from L to R as row 1.
K 1 row MC. Bring needle 4 forward and lay in col B, working from R to L as row 1.
K 1 row MC. Bring needle 3 forward and lay in col B, working from R to L as row 1.
K 1 row MC. Bring needle 2 forward and lay in col B, working from R to L.
Repeat from *.

DESIGN 16

Tension 3
Cotton main yarn with chunky space-dyed wool laying-in yarn
Cast on 4 sts: 1, 2, 3 and 4.

*K 1 row MC (cotton), bring needle 1 forward, but be careful to keep the st over the latch. Lay col B (chunky) (fancy yarn or knitted tube) into the hook of the needle, working from R to L.
K 1 row MC, bring needle 2 forward and lay in col B, working from L to R as row 1.

K 1 row MC, bring needle 3 forward and lay in col B, working from L to R as row 1.
K 1 row MC, bring needle 4 forward and lay in col B, working from L to R as row 1.
K 1 row MC, bring needle 3 forward and lay in col B, working from R to L as row 1.
K 1 row MC, bring needle 2 forward and lay in col B, working from R to L as row 1.
Repeat from *.

DESIGN 17

Tension 2
Cotton main colour with lurex cord laying-in yarn

1 cord in lurex (to knit this see braid pattern 9).

Cast on 2 sts: 1 and 2.
*K 1 row MC (cotton), then take the st from needle 1 onto transfer tool and place cord behind the st, working from R to L. Replace st on needle.
K 1 row MC, then take the st from needle 2 onto transfer tool and place cord behind the st, working from L to R. Replace st on needle.
Repeat from *.

DESIGN 18

Multiples of 3 stitches/Tension 5
100% cotton or any straight yarn

Cast on as many sts as you require the length of the edging to be, in a waste yarn. K 10-15 rows. Change to MC.
K 6 rows, then transfer every 3rd st to next needle on R and leave the empty needles in WP.
K 6 rows, then pick up the loops from 1st row of MC and replace on needles directly above, being careful to pick up every stitch.
K 2 rows, then cast off with MC.
Take off waste yarn.

DESIGN 19

Tension 7
100% Wool
6 stitches worked over 9 needles, needles numbered 1, 2, 3, 4, 5, 6, 7, 8 and 9

Cast on 6 sts on needles 1, 2, 3, 4, 5 and 6. Leave needles 7, 8 and 9 in NWP.
*K 6 rows, then push needles 7, 8 and 9 into WP.
Using a 3-pronged transfer tool, take sts from needles 1, 2 and 3 and hook them onto needles 7, 8 and 9. The st from needle 1 is now on needle 7, the st from needle 2 is now on needle 8 and the st from needle 3 is now on needle 9. Push needles 1, 2 and 3 to NWP.
K 6 rows, then push needles 1, 2 and 3 into WP.
Using a 3-pronged transfer tool, take sts from needles 7, 8 and 9 and hook them onto needles 1, 2 and 3. The st from needle 7 is now on needle 1, the st from needle 8 is now on needle 2 and the st from needle 9 is now on needle 3. Push needles 7, 8 and 9 to NWP.
Repeat from *.

DESIGN 20

Multiples of 2 sts/Tension 4
100% Lurex or any straight yarn

Cast on as many sts as you require the length of the edging to be in a waste yarn. K 10-15 rows. Change feeder to MC (lurex).
K 7 rows, then transfer every other st to next needle on R and leave empty needles in WP.
K 7 rows, then pick up the loops from 1st row of MC and replace on needles directly above, being careful to pick up every st.
K 2 rows, then cast off with MC. Take off waste yarn.

DESIGN 21

Tension 5
Needle set-out 1·1111····11
100% Wool

Cast on 7 sts following the needle set-out and start knitting.
*K 4 rows, then cable the group of 4 sts. Pick up 2 sts on L of the group with 1st transfer tool. Pick up 2 sts on R of the group with 2nd transfer tool and put these onto the 2 empty needles on L. Cross the 2 sts from L over the 2 sts from R and put them onto the 2 empty needles on R.
This forms the cable repeat from *.

DESIGN 22

Tension 4
Cotton main yarn with lurex tape laying-in yarn

Cast on 5 sts: 1, 2, 3, 4 and 5.
*K 2 rows MC (cotton).
Pull needle 4 out, but be careful not to take the st over the latch, and lay the fancy yarn over the needle, working from L to R.
K 2 rows.
Pull out needle 2 and lay the fancy yarn over it as before, but working from R to L.
Repeat from *.

This is a versatile design because any yarn can be used and the design can be changed easily by adding sts at the sides or in the middle of those in the instructions.

An even more drastic change can be achieved by adding more rows between laying in the fancy yarn.

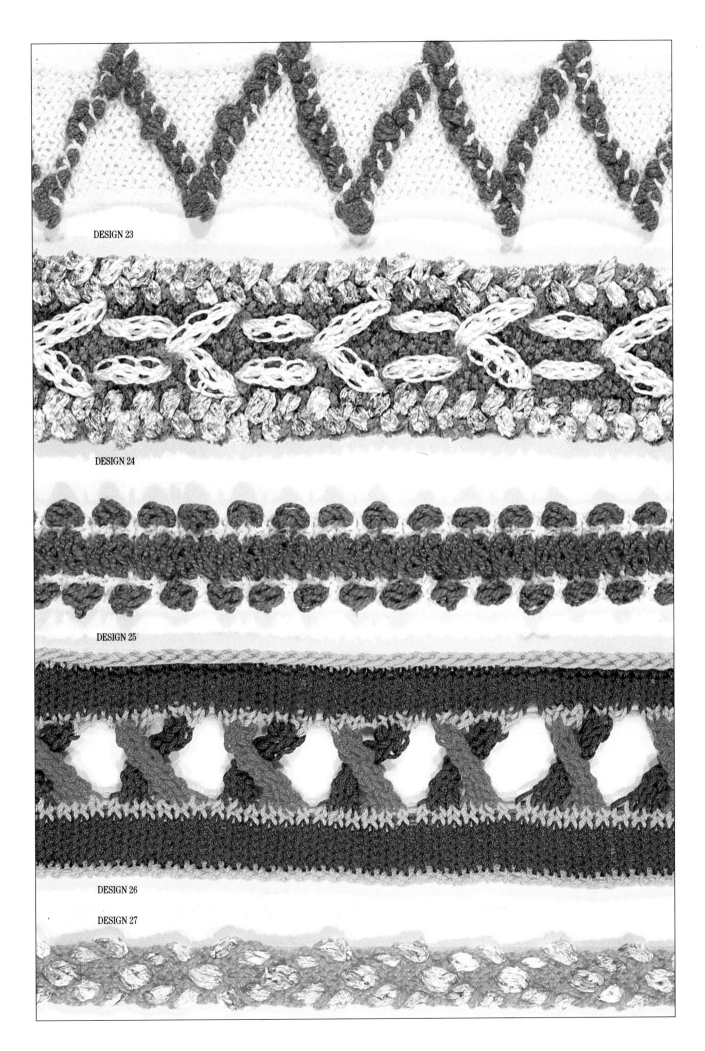

DESIGN 23

DESIGN 24

DESIGN 25

DESIGN 26

DESIGN 27

DESIGN 23

Tension 6
Cotton gimp main yarn with cotton cord laying-in yarn

1 tube in cotton (to knit this see braid pattern 9)

Cast on 10 sts: 1, 2, 3, 4, 5, 6, 7, 8, 9 and 10.
K 1 row MC (cotton gimp), bring needle 1 forward, but be careful to keep the st over the latch, and lay col B (blue) into the hook of the needle, working from R to L.
*K 1 row MC, then bring needle 2 forward and lay in col B, working from L to R.
Repeat from * with needles 3, 4, 5, 6, 7, 8, 9 and 10.
**K 1 row MC, then bring needle 9 forward and lay in col B, working from R to L.
Repeat from ** with needles 8, 7, 6, 5, 4, 3, 2 and 1.
Repeat from 1st *.

DESIGN 24

Tension 8
Chenille main yarn and rayon cords

K cords A and B col A (multi-colour) and cords C and D col B (grey rayon) (to knit this see pattern 9).

Cast on 12 sts: 1, 2, 3, 4, 5, 6, 7, 8, 9, 10, 11 and 12.
Row 1: K 1 row MC (chenille), then take st from needle 3 and place cord A behind the st, working from L to R, then replace st. Place cord B behind st on needle 10, working from R to L. Place cord C behind st on needle 4 working R to L and cord D behind st on needle 9, working from L to R.
Row 2: K 1 row MC. Place cord A behind st on needle 1, working from R to L and cord B behind st on needle 12, working from L to R.
Row 3: K 1 row MC. Place cord A behind st on needle 3, working from L to R and cord B behind st on needle 10 working from R to L.
Row 4: Work as row 2.
Row 5: Work as row 3.
Row 6: K 1 row MC. Place cord A behind st on needle 1, working from R to L, and cord B behind st on needle 12, working from L to R. Place cord C behind st on needle 6, working from L to R. Place cord D behind st on needle 7, working from R to L.
Row 7: Work as row 3.
Row 8: Work as row 2.
Row 9: Work as row 3.
Row 10: Work as row 2.
Row 11: K 1 row MC. Place cord A behind st on needle 3, working from L to R and cord B behind st on needle 10, working from R to L. Place cord C behind st on needle 9, working from L to R. Place cord D behind st on needle 4, working from R to L.
Tubes C and D will now have crossed over.
Row 12: Work as row 2.
Row 13: Work as row 3.
Row 14: Work as row 2.
Row 15: Work as row 3.
Row 16: K 1 row MC. Place cord A behind st on needle 1, working from R to L, and cord B behind st on needle 3, working from L to R. Place cord C behind st on needle 7, working from R to L. Place cord D behind st on needle 6, working from L to R.
Row 17: Work as row 3.
Row 18: Work as row 2.
Row 19: Work as row 3.
Row 20: Work as row 2.
Repeat from row 1.

DESIGN 25

Tension 6
Cotton gimp, main yarn; cotton cord

K 1 tube cotton (see braid pattern 9).

Cast on 7 sts: 1, 2, 3, 4, 5, 6 and 7.
*K 2 rows MC (cotton gimp), then take st from needle 2 and place cord behind the st, working from L to R. Replace st on needle and take st from needle 6 and place cord behind the st, working from L to R. Replace st on needle.
K 2 rows MC, then take st from needle 6 and place cord behind the st, working from R to L. Replace st on needle, then take st from needle 2 and place cord behind the st, working from R to L. Replace st on needle.
Repeat from *.

DESIGN 26

Tension 6
Mercerised cotton

Cast on as many sts as you require the length of braid to be in col A (yellow), using closed-edge method. K 2 rows.
K 6 rows col B (navy).
K 2 rows col A.

Push all needles into HP, set for Hold. Carriage on R.
*Push 1st 3 needles on R into WP, K 10 rows col B. Push these 3 needles into HP and push the 3 needles next to them into WP, K 10 rows in col C (pink).
Repeat from * until you have completed the width of knitting.
**Push the 1st set of 6 needles into WP and with transfer tools transfer the 3 sts from L set of 3 needles onto R set and R 3 sts onto L set of needles (ie, col B over col C). Repeat from ** across the knitting.
All needles should now be in WP.
K 2 rows col A.
K 6 rows col B.
K 1 row col A.
Cast off with col A.

DESIGN 27

Tension 2

This braid can be knitted with any straight yarn and fancy yarn or as illustrated here using 2 knitted cords in rayon and cotton main yarn.

Cast on 5 sts: 1, 2, 3, 4 and 5.
*K 2 rows col A (pink).
Take the st from needle 1 and place cord A behind the st, working from R to L.
Replace st on needle.
Take the st from needle 5 and place cord B behind the st, working from L to R.
Replace st on needle.
K 2 rows col A.
Now lay cord A behind the st on needle 2, working from L to R, and cord B behind the st on needle 4, working from R to L.
K 2 rows col A.
Now lay cord A behind the st on needle 4, working from L to R, and cord B behind the st on needle 2, working from R to L.*
This forms repeat 1. Repeat 2 is the same, but the colours are reversed. These 2 complete repeats form the total pattern from * to *.

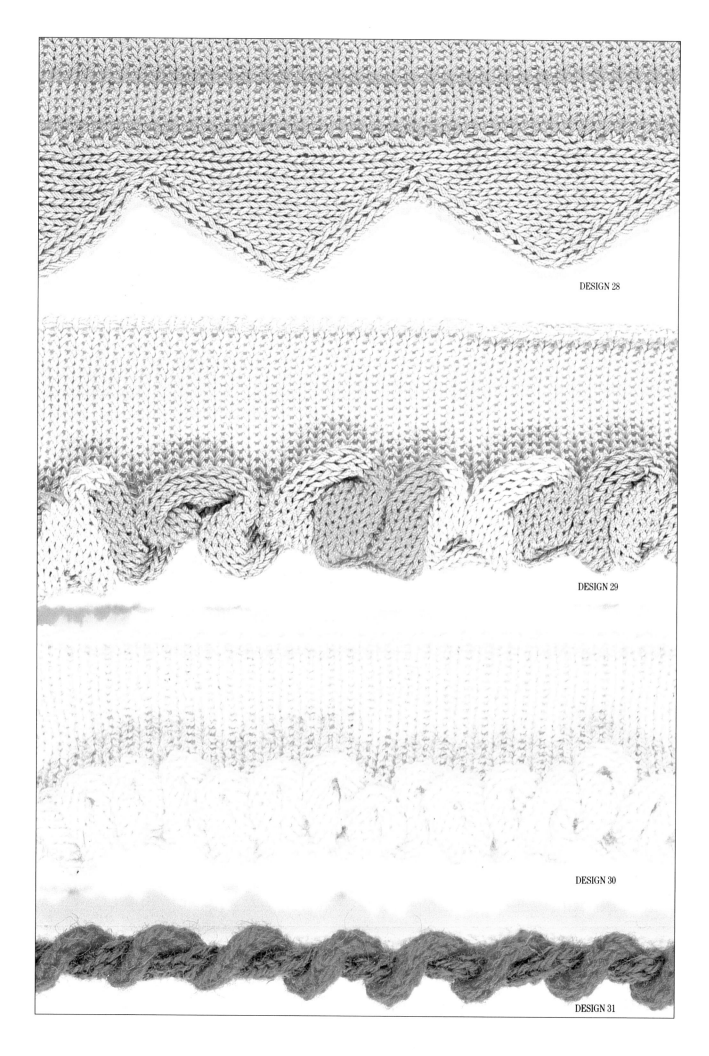

DESIGN 28

DESIGN 29

DESIGN 30

DESIGN 31

DESIGN 28

Tension 6
Mercerised cotton

Pattern worked over 12 needles, needles numbered 1, 2, 3, 4, 5, 6, 7, 8, 9, 10, 11 and 12

Using col A (grey), cast on over needles 1, 2, 3, 4 and 5, carriage on R. Keep needles 6, 7, 8, 9, 10, 11 and 12 in NWP.
*K 2 rows, increase 1 stitch (see note).
Repeat from * until all 12 needles are in WP.
**K 2 rows, decrease 1 stitch (see note). Repeat from ** until only 5 needles are in WP.
Repeat from 1st * until border is required length. Cast off.
    Now pick up the straight edge of the border and replace on the machine with the pearl edge fac-

ing outwards. To ensure neatness, do not pick up the very end loops but the 2nd row of loops on the K side.
K 2 rows col B (pink).
K 4 rows col A.
K 2 rows col B.
Continue with main garment.

Note
To increase: using a 3-pronged transfer tool, pick up the last 3 sts on R and move them over 1 needle to R. To fill the empty needle, pick up the loop from the bottom of st on R and hook over empty needle.
To decrease: using a 3-pronged transfer tool, pick up the last 3 sts on R and move them over 1 needle to L. Push the empty needle into the NWP.

DESIGN 29

Tension 6
Mercerised cotton

9 sts, needles numbered 1, 2, 3, 4, 5, 6, 7, 8 and 9
Cast on col A (beige).
*K 16 rows, pick up right edge of knitting and hook onto needles 1 and 5.
K 16 rows, pick up left edge of knitting and hook onto needles 5

and 9.
    This forms the repeat from *. Change colour after every 2 repeats. When edging is required length, cast off.
    Now hook edging back onto the machine widthways along the straight edge.
    Continue with main garment.

DESIGN 30

Tension 6
Cotton gimp

6 stitches, needles numbered 1, 2, 3, 4, 5 and 6
Cast on. *K 10 rows, pick up right edge of knitting and hook onto needles 1 and 3.
K 10 rows, pick up left edge of knitting and hook onto needles 4

and 6.
Repeat from * until edging is required length.
Cast off.
Now hook edging back onto the machine widthways along the straight edge. Continue with main garment.

DESIGN 31

Tension 5
Shetland wool

This braid is made from cords. To make these, refer to pattern 9.

This braid requires 2 cords of different colours, eg red and green.

This braid is produced by attaching the cords while knitting the braid. This is done by picking up loops from the cords and hooking them onto needles.

Cast on 5 sts in MC (white) and hook the 2 cords onto the needles by one of their loops, col A (green) on L and col B (red) on R of the 5 needles being used.
*K 2 rows MC.
Take cord B and hook onto centre needle.
K 2 rows MC.
Take cord A and hook onto centre needle.
K 2 rows MC.
Take cord B over cord A and hook onto outside needle on R.
K 2 rows MC.
Take cord A over cord B and hook onto outside needle on L.
Repeat from *.

FRINGES

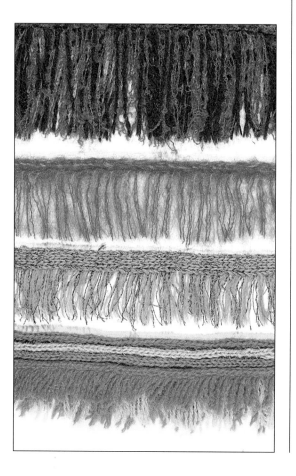

All fringes illustrated are knitted by using the same technique. The method is as follows:

Needle set-out 11·········111

Cast on, taking the yarn as a long float from 1st set of needles to the 2nd set. K 1-2in (25-50mm), which will allow you to see the fringe uncut as illustrated. If your tension is too loose you will have a very thin fringe. Rectify this by tightening your tension as much as possible – the tighter you knit, the more tightly packed the floats will be and the richer your fringe.

To produce the fringes as illustrated, you simply rearrange the original needle set out. The closer you bring the sets of needles in the WP, the shorter the float and fringe. Some very short uncut fringes are shown as these can be very attractive and useful as edgings and bindings. Fringes can be used together, by laying them one on top of another to give a multi-layered look. Try using a number of fine ends of yarn together, mixing textured yarns with plain. Such combinations can give wonderfully rich results.

Many variations are possible and only a few are shown. Try creating your own ideas by increasing the number of needles in work at one side. This increases the rolled edge which holds the cut fringe together, or try striping colours into the fringe.

OTHER DECORATIVE TECHNIQUES

APPLYING BEADS

There are a number of different methods for applying beads to knitting. This one enables the knitter to use a large range of beads in different sizes and shapes.

Thread all the beads on any strong fine yarn. Push needles forward. Lay the yarn threaded with beads over and under alternate needles pulling the beads into the desired position. They will obviously have to be under the needles the yarn is not going over, as they must allow the carriage to pass over them without interference. Knit the next row with care then, if necessary, pull the yarn threaded with beads to tighten them on the knitting.

SWISS DARNING OR EMBROIDERY

Bring a threaded needle up through the knitting at the bottom of a stitch. Then take the needle up and down through the bottom of the next stitch above, bringing the yarn out on the other side. Now bring the needle through as near as possible to where you first brought it up through the knitting. Pull the thread gently and, as it tightens, it will form a second stitch over the original one, changing its colour to that of the thread you are using. Swiss darning can be used to great effect on many designs and is used extensively in modern sweaters.

MILLING AND FELTING

Wool is the only yarn which can be changed by this method of finishing. The easiest way to felt knitting is to place the fabric into an automatic washing machine and give it a standard colour wash. Pure soap must be used, not detergent. Felting can also be done by hand; use as little really hot water as possible and with pure soap rub the knitting vigorously until felting takes place, usually about 8-10 minutes. If rubber gloves are worn, much hotter water can be used which causes felting to take place more quickly.

ABBREVIATIONS

MC	main colour	L	left
col	colour	R	right
HP	hold position	Ø	central position on
NWP	non working position		machine needle bed
UWP	upper working position	st(s)	stitch(es)
WP	working position	T	tension
K	knit	LH	left hand
KC I	(dial positions on Brother	RH	right hand
KC II	(machines		

ACKNOWLEDGEMENTS

I would like to thank the David & Charles team for all the consideration shown me during the production of this book, especially my editor Pam Griffiths whose advice was always readily available. I wish to thank Mary Davis who had the unenviable job of checking all the patterns and did so patiently and without a harsh word. Many thanks to Derby Lonsdale College textile department, who gave me support and assistance, particularly staff members Shelley North and Lesley Marlow. The following students contributed and worked some of the designs: Zou Akroyd, Louise Cartwright, Jane Puddy, Karen Jennings, Andrew Darbyshire, Chen Ip, Susan Hales, Jackie Walsh, Corinne Lambert, Andrea Palmer and Amanda King. Thanks have to be given to Freddie Robins and Sophie Steller, who assisted in my studio and particular thanks to Heather Stewart, who was a tower of strength and without whom the book would never have been finished on time. Finally my thanks to a dear friend Melanie Miller who so carefully compiled the index.

The book has been a mammoth job of designing, writing and knitting, an enormous job made possible by the very generous help of all mentioned.

INDEX

Entries in **bold** refer to main stitch sections